I0201823

The Girl That God Fell To

A woman's visions of God & His Army of Light saving souls.

And how a deceased nun, petitioned for beatification, helped Him do it.

Irene A. Lawlor

A Life Dream Publishing Book

© Copyright Irene Lawlor 2024

The right of Irene Lawlor to be identified as the author of this work has been asserted in accordance with The Copyright and Related Rights Act, 2000.

Condition of Sale

This book is sold subject to the conditions that it will not, by way of commercial transaction or otherwise, be offered for the use of a third party, or for any activity other than for the personal use of the purchaser, or lent, re-sold, hired or otherwise circulated in any form other than that for which it is published and without a similar condition including this condition being imposed on the subsequent purchaser.

Life Dream Publishing, Ireland

lifedreampublishing@gmail.com

In memory of Mother Yvonne-Aimée of Jesus

Table Of Contents

Preface

Irish woman Helena Carroll was a typical housewife, mother, and sister who led an ordinary life in north county Dublin. After her husband and children, the love of her life was her horse, who she rode out each day around the nearby fields and beaches. Like many people, Helena had her ups and downs, but she maintained a positive outlook.

In September 2019, the 43-year-old took up meditation to help her relax and adopt a more sanguine approach to her daily life. Her meditative ability would change her life forever, taking her on a nine-month out of body, ethereal odyssey where she came face to face with God, His heavenly congregation, and the spirits of some of history's most famous leaders. What started as a meditation practice for her, opened a connection which led to the eventual descension of these spirits on the mother of two, which lasted for a period of nine months. Among these spirits were, Henry VIII, Queen Elizabeth I, Catherine the Great, Martin Luther King, and a French nun, Sr. Yvonne Beauvais. They appeared to her under God's command to do a job and bring a message - *the world is in trouble.*

As Elizabeth I warned, *"What I say is true time and time again; The planet you're on, it will be at an end.* While Henry VIII added, *"I pray, I pray, I pray; he has something to say. I'm here, and I have never gone away. I still rule from above here. We still all work for He you see; We are all still here, still here within the Light."*

There would also be a battle. A spiritual battle of light against dark, overseen by Catherine the Great who informed us, *"We will fight once more you see, but we will all be fighting for He.*

For He is the creator of all, and we have heard His call. Rounded us all up, one by one to get the job done, right or wrong there will be a storm, a storm from the heavens you will see; this will be." This

1

Irish woman is my sister Helena, and she was also chosen to do Gods will.

Helena didn't know why these events were happening, but thankfully she described and recorded her experience's daily, allowing us to tell this story. She could never have imagined that Spirit, with their eternal patience, had been waiting for her since the age of eighteen to turn her attention inward. Eventually at the age of forty-three she began to meditate, enjoying beautiful visions of sacred images - images, which I hadn't realized at the time were so vivid and real. The cinema in her mind kept her enthralled, while I wondered how she took to meditation so easily, when others found it quite difficult. It wasn't until she explained to me, just how detailed these visions were, that I began to believe something extraordinary was happening. Then, when she felt something connect in her mind, and was introduced to her spirit guide Luther, who sat on a throne, we knew something inconceivable was happening to her.

Luther taught Helena how to release deceased earthbound spirits into the Light - spirits of people who never made it to their eternal resting place. We believed she was becoming a powerful medium and were light-hearted and happy. We couldn't have realized the seriousness of the job that she was to do, how much work it would involve, or how exhausted she would become. Neither could we have known or conceived of what would unfold for us over the following nine months.

Luther said to Helena, *"We have known each other before. You are the reincarnated soul of Sr. Yvonne Beauvais. She lives again in you. She is in your soul."* Searching the internet, we were shocked to find this French Augustinian nun existed! It was Yvonne's work that Helena was to do. You see, Yvonne's desire was to save souls and it seems Jesus had granted Yvonne her wish, and that was only the beginning, because Yvonne was not alone – heaven came with her.

This book reads like a fantastic work of fiction, but for my sister and I the events she experienced seemed very real. If it compels you to believe it, it's probably because it's so unbelievable, few people would have the audacity to make it up. Because of the diversity and duration of the experiences and the fast, fluent and at times eloquent channels she dictated she neither had the intellectual ability or educational acumen to do so. I say this with the greatest respect for my sister. In fact, Helena has had life-long learning difficulties, and the only books she owns are her children's. I invite you to read this book with both an open mind and healthy scepticism and decide for yourself if it is indeed fact or fiction.

These events occurred between September 2019 and July 2020 and were recorded daily on WhatsApp audio and text messages, from which I am writing this book. It's been a lonely journey, because we spoke of it only to a couple of family members whose subtle scepticism made us retreat into silence. During this time Helena and I went about our daily lives. As a result of these experiences, Helena's mental health deteriorated rapidly and within four weeks of the cessation of events, she was admitted to the Ashlin Centre, Beaumont Hospital in Dublin; a facility for people with mental health issues, where she stayed for two weeks. Back to normal life, Helena, her husband, and I are the only people who know that something rather incredible happened to her.

The Beginning

Background

Helena and I come from Dublin, Ireland, and grew up with five other siblings. Together, we are four girls and three boys. We were raised Roman Catholic, attending mass weekly when growing up and less as we grew older, raising our children catholic as well. However, we cannot describe ourselves as ever being deeply religious. My name is Irene, and I'm one of Helena's three older sisters. I am married and have four daughters. Helena is the youngest girl in the family and has two sons. There's nothing extraordinary about our family; we were all born and lived in the same house that my father lives in today. My father told us ghost stories throughout our childhood, some of which my mother and relations corroborated, and so we always believed in a 'spirit world.' (In a channel with Luther, Helena was told that God wanted her to start her spiritual work at the age of eighteen, but Helena wasn't ready). As I wrote this book, I began to link Luther's revelation with the spiritual activity our family experienced in the nineties around the time Helena turned eighteen; events I believed were inexplicable - until now.

Around 1993, this phenomenon began with a feeling that someone unseen was in the room. We felt an 'energy' or a 'pins and needles' sensation. Footsteps were heard when no one else was in the house. We'd watch a keyring move in our kitchen door with nothing obvious moving it while biscuit wrappers crinkled and moved of their own accord. One night, lying in bed, Helena heard a thud, and the house shook - a rush of energy raced to her bedroom as if an aggressive man ran to attack her, his presence stopped by her bed. Every night around midnight, this presence held her down, and Helena, unable to move, screamed inside, but no one could hear. She told our parents, who paid little attention or didn't know what to do. Afraid, she spent most of her nights awake and luckily had a job that began at noon.

My siblings and friends experienced this spiritual activity. My sister Theresa, a diabetic, became unwell from its effects, grew weaker, and collapsed. Then, my parents took the situation seriously. It's a long time ago, so the details are forgotten, but they found a healing group who prayed over Theresa until she became better. But this negative spirit returned nightly for years. A friend, Barbara, saw a man wearing a long dark coat pass our kitchen window and opened the door to welcome him. She was surprised to find no one there. My brother's wife, Deirdre, also had a story from the night she slept in our family home. She said, "While asleep in bed, I woke twice with intense pressure on my chest – the second time, an old woman with long grey hair wearing a white night dress stood at the foot of my bed. Her presence calmed me, and the pressure lifted quickly."

Cathal, my brother, also experienced this pressure, but he witnessed the torso of a man holding him down. On another occasion, while I was living in America, my brother Thomas visited, and I woke from sleep feeling a great force holding me down. I screamed but wasn't heard by my boyfriend lying beside me. After three nights, this spirit, who had accompanied my brother, left. Since then, when alone, I sleep with the light on. These nightly events were so bad at times that my sisters climbed into my parent's bed, and our father wrapped them in his arms to protect them. The girls seemed vulnerable, while my dad, a builder, was a huge man. On one memorable night, Helena tells this story, "Dad was shielding us from a negative energy that was creeping up from the bottom of his bed. As it moved closer, we felt a push-back from positive energy at the top of the bed as if we were being protected. There was a battle between two spiritual forces; the energies were so strong it felt as though the mattress was breathing."

We attempted to rid the house of spirits and called various mediums, one of which was a regular on a Dublin radio station, but nobody could help. Priests blessed our house and its occupants, but the spirits remained. Over the years, the activity subsided, but there was always a presence around Helena, which was the case when she visited me on my return from America. My husband and I went to bed on that occasion, leaving Helena downstairs with her boyfriend. I was woken by somebody grabbing my arm and shaking it roughly. Dazed, I opened my eyes, and seeing no one, I drifted back to sleep, only to be grabbed again by this anxious spirit. Helena cried out, and

6

I ran downstairs to find her boyfriend had hit her; we threw him out. Looking back now, with the incident in our parents' bedroom, the lady at the bottom of Deirdre's bed, the man at the kitchen window, and this protective spirit, it looked like there were both negative and positive spirits around Helena. In retrospect, it seems some spirits waited for her to begin her spiritual work while others offered protection.

Helena is eight years my junior, likes a smoke and a drink, and for years was the life and soul of a party. She has a good heart and is extremely hard-working. When the Irish economy collapsed, her husband lost his job. This, compounded by high rental costs and a baby due, made saving for a deposit on a new house impossible. The living conditions in a tiny two-bed cottage were stifling. Her cottage sits in the large back garden of our ancestral home. Her learning difficulties and low self-esteem placed her in physically demanding jobs, adding to her body's wear and tear. Her combined fibromyalgia (a chronic disorder causing widespread pain and stiffness) and scoliosis (curvature of the spine) left her in severe pain, and at times she needed help turning in bed. She retired from work in the catering industry as it became too much for her. She felt trapped and lost hope of ever making it to a house of her own. In September 2019, I suggested Helena eat a healthier diet, exercise regularly, and meditate; for once, she listened. Helena didn't know anything about meditation, so I advised her to watch YouTube videos. This was the first time Helena sat still in her life, *and that is when it all began.*

In a message given by an Angel of the Lord, God said:

"The heavens will fall today; they are on their way.
The earth is in trouble, Helena, in a big, big way.
God is not happy with the way it's run today.
Greed and poverty are all over, you see,
and a change needs to be made before the world ends, you see.
God will come down through you,
and you will let the world see that God did fall to ye.

The Year 2019

Visions, Guides & Spirits

Spiritual Chiropractors

In September, Helena began to meditate while sitting cross-legged on her kitchen floor. Wearing an eye mask normally used for sleep, she saw beautiful swirling colours blending from emerald- green to purple and then orange to red; simultaneously, her body began to rotate anti-clockwise. Asking if that happened to me, I replied, "No," but I wanted her to develop a practice, so I said go with the-flow. I thought she might be getting a bit 'caught up' in this new beginning, but as long as she practiced, I didn't care. Helena said, "It was cool; I might do that again."

In October, while watching the colours, Helena felt herself rising out of her body while looking down on the individual rooms of her cottage, which were getting smaller. Coming back into her body, she voiced-mailed, saying, "Irene, what was all that about?" I told her it sounded like an out-of-body experience. She had never heard of it before. Soon after, she began to see very clear mind pictures,' some of which were the face of a wolf, a lamb with a bad leg, and snowcapped mountains. I told her they were just thoughts and to ignore them. I hadn't realized just how clear these pictures were.

October 25th: While meditating with her hands in the prayer position, her body started rotating, and she felt pressure on her upper back and neck that pushed her forward until she faced the floor. It was as though she was being stretched and pulled, and pain moved through her knees, hips, and spine. Sitting up, she raised her hands in the air to stretch, then restored them to the prayer position. Again, she felt herself being pulled to the ground, her face once again staring at the floor. The pressure continued moving through her back, neck, and head. She felt it in her nose, teeth, and even in her tongue, which started to tingle. Her hands, still in prayer, began opening finger by finger and stretching outward. She said, *"It's weird; I let it all happen; maybe my body just needed to stretch out, especially my back and my lopsided hips.* " Her body started to rotate again, this time in small semicircles to the left. *"It pulled again and again to the left, then pushed me forward, then semicircles to the left and pushed me forward, then semicircles to the left and pushed me forward repeatedly until my face reached the ground."* I listened to Helena's voicemail and was shocked. That would terrify me, but Helena thought it was part of meditation and asked if anything like that happened to me. I was surprised she believed this was normal.

October 27th: Sitting on her kitchen floor, Helena's neck was manipulated by an invisible chiropractor. It was adjusted to the left, then around and around to the left again, cracking out the tension in her neck, and then it suddenly stopped. A couple of minutes later, the process was repeated on the right. Some unseen force was manipulating her again. She noticed the colours in her mind's eye brightening like this movement had unblocked something. Laughing on the phone, she quipped, "As a chiropractic session, it was worth at least sixty euros."

I didn't want to scare Helena, but she didn't understand that this was profound. She said, "It felt good and was a great experience." Helena had a horse called Belle, and the previous day, she'd mucked out her stable, which exacerbated her neck pain. The day after the manipulation, her pain and stiffness were gone. I have to say I was a little envious. I had been meditating on and off for years, and the most I felt was a gentle stream of energy and a few minor psychic impressions. I never experienced anything like that. She didn't realize that everyone didn't experience out-of-body experiences and spirit chiropractors, but when I thought about it, I realized it was the first time she'd ever meditated, and it happened so fast. How was she to believe this didn't happen to everyone?

October 30th: During meditation, Helena saw a 'sheet of white light' flash twice across her mind's eye, accompanied by pressure, like something locked and connected in her forehead. Her right hand rose by itself, moved toward her abdomen, and rested there.

The Teachers

November 12th: I received a voicemail from Helena, who said, "I was relaxing when I heard a woman's voice whisper, "Helena, we are teachers." The hairs stood on my neck. I'm not going to lie; it was a very exciting day for me. I suspected spirits might be trying to communicate, and Helena might become a channel or a medium. With her eyes closed, she described seeing a type of movie screen, and to the bottom left and top right of this 'screen,' tiny lights flickered. She said, "I know when I see them, I am going deeper and deeper." She alternated her meditation positions, sometimes sitting upright and lying down more frequently. She was surprised to hear herself conversing with someone she didn't know. The following day, Helena had a vision of me walking through a door. I'm smiling and radiant like the sun is shining through me. She's shown sacred books and heard the word 'scriptures.' Suddenly, she's jolted awake with a deep breath, her spine lifting off the bed. She described it as a baby being born and taking its first breath. I wondered if she had left her body and if her spirit was jumping back in. That night, as she slept, she heard herself answering someone, "No, I can't talk to you. I am too tired. I will talk to you another time." Then she felt herself sinking into her body.

Third Eye and the Realm

Saturday, November 16th: I woke late to a voicemail from Helena who said, "Irene, call me as soon as you get this." The previous night, she'd felt a presence beside her. She spoke to it, saying, "Look, there is no point in standing there. I don't know how to communicate with you, and I'm tired." It left, and she went to sleep. When she woke, her presence was there again. She blinked, then closed her eyes and saw a blazing lime green light; it was very bright against a black space. The light swirled around and around and formed an eye. She opened her eyes, and the room filled with the lime-green color, as if this 'eye' was projecting out into the room or she was seeing around her with a new type of vision. The eye looked like a human eye with full eyelashes. Its pupil was black, but the iris was lime green. Through the pupil of this 'eye,' she saw a realm and a swirling cloud of neon colours within it. Helena described the realm as looking into 'deep space' or a 'night sky.' She covered her eyes to block out exterior light; instantly, Helena was there; she was in the realm. A vibrant pink spirit floated towards her, pulsating and waving like jellyfish filmed in the dark ocean. Helena sensed it was female and said, "Hello! Thank you so much." Helena felt she had been given a gift. Practical matters arose, and she excused herself, saying, "I have to go, but I will come back to you." Helena voice-mailed again, "Wow, Irene! Wow! Wow! Wow! I can't wait for you to wake up."

After breakfast, Helena closed her eyes and found herself back in the realm, having another incredible experience: a vision of a lorry jack-knifing and coming straight towards her. Strong vibrations shook her body as if the lorry skidded into her. She felt herself lying in a rescue helicopter and became acutely aware of her heart. Sharp pains shot through her torso as if being resuscitated. A date was impressed on her mind when she heard a song and realized the initials of the singer were the same as the person in the accident.

I immediately looked up the information on the internet and found the exact details Helena had described. The accident happened in the countryside, and the person, a lady, was airlifted to hospital. I forwarded the newspaper article to Helena on WhatsApp, and as she read it, she felt energy surge through her body. The spirit of the lady stood beside her, wanting Helena to know that it was *her* in the article. When Helena closed her eyes, she saw and felt the spirit of this lady in the realm. This is how Helena described it, "It's as if I'm wearing a virtual reality headset; I can be totally immersed in that realm while interacting with people in the physical world; I have access to both places at the same time."

The following day, more detailed information was given, which we verified on the internet. Helena had gotten everything right. Through a multi-sensory experience, this lady made Helena experience every aspect of her death. That night, as Helena slept, she had a vivid dream were our brother announced his mother-in-law was deceased – and simultaneously, an orb floated in front of him. This 'dream' suggested that the orb was her spirit. The dream's intention was to illustrate that spirits took the form of orbs. As time went by, I learned that everything that happened to Helena came with an introduction, either in visions or through verbal communication, thus showing an *order* to these events. Over the following weeks, many spirits connected with Helena, providing details of their deaths, some of which we verified on the internet. Thus, confirming to us that Helena had mediumship abilities. It was designed to do just that! Encouraging us to believe and be receptive to what would unfold.

Night of Terror

November 18th: Helena lay with earphones on, listening to soft music, but was disappointed that nothing was happening. Then she described experiencing 'a suction noise' and could hardly hear the music anymore, like her mind was in a quieter place. She had clarity, which stayed with her throughout the day. That night, Helena regretted wishing for more. Numerous spirits impressed upon her the events of their lives and deaths. Some whispered while others banged on the bed, looking for attention. At one stage, Helena felt herself lowered into a grave and heard dirt thrown on top of the coffin. The pressure at the back of her head was tremendous. She was angry and told them all to leave. She heard their favorite songs - everything from Madonna to Irish folk songs. One man asked her to meet him on the "26th of November at 10:45 am," as if he were an executive scheduling an appointment. Terrified, she messaged the following morning, saying, "Irene, I think I need help; I don't know how to control this, and I can't have another night like this. They are trying to make appointments now." I laughed at the idea, but it wasn't funny. I don't know how she got through that night. For the first time in my life, I wondered: if I was given this 'gift,' would I take it?

The next day, we called a medium who advised Helena to receive Reiki healing and recommended a local lady to do it. After the session, Helena slept like a baby, but it also triggered within me a memory: about nine years previous, after I had a heart-attack, I received a healing from an Irish Bio Energy healer. I felt much better after and decided to take one of his courses, *Healing for Family and Friends*. I practiced on my daughters and Helena. After Helena's healing, she said, "Irene, I saw all these colored lights swirling around, I am lightheaded and dizzy. Wow! That was amazing!" She spoke excitedly after her experience, but I thought she was exaggerating, so I dismissed it. I wonder if I might have unintentionally begun activating something within her.

In the space of a few months, Helena had experienced Clairsentience Clairaudience, opened her third eye, had an out-of-body experience, and met a spiritual being. I had never heard of anyone having so many combined spiritual experiences. The following morning, she went to feed her horse, Belle, and saw a vaporous cloud of tiny sparkles in the air. They came floating towards her like dandelion seedlings. Later, though afraid, she meditated and was surprised to see that her third eye had changed dramatically. Instead of a black pupil and green iris, there was a red circle framed by a gold circle, like the sun shining behind it. The gold then changed to orange. She watched it for a while and was a little freaked out, so she tried to clear her mind but again saw the wolf walking towards her. Helena thought she was being tutored while she slept, because waking during the night, felt like she was taking a lunch break. What the subject was, she didn't know.

Visions of Jesus

It was the early hours of the morning of November 22nd when Helena woke in the realm. On her screen were images of angel's wings, sacred books, and Jesus on the crucifix - tears dropping from his eyes. Then her head was pulled back sharply, and with great power, it hurt as something crunched inside. A quiet voice spoke to her; the only words she heard were, "While you sleep." She said, "I don't care what anyone thinks, Irene. I know that this was God speaking to me."

Spirits Request Help

November 27th: Helena was horse riding after having a quiet night with plenty of sleep – she was in good form. I received a voice message, *"Irene, I'm looking around and seeing a haze of colours like heat waves in the air. They're like a rainbow coming directly at me from the clouds."* Later, lying down, she fell into a relaxed state when suddenly the lady in her vision, who had been struck by the lorry, confronted her in the realm, wanting to know where Helena had been. Then, more people confronted her while handing her cards. She remembered telling them she couldn't take them all together; it would have to be one at a time. She promised someone, *"Yes, I will do you first."* Helena wasn't sure what she was to do, but they were anxious for her help.

Third Eye Change

December 1st: Helena woke to darkness and found herself looking into a pupil. Only as the eye blinked and moved away from her did she realize it was the pupil of the 'third eye.' We realized that as she woke, her third eye opened a second later (like camera lenses adjusting to light, it adjusted itself also and now seemed further out in space.) We also began to realize that the third eye was both a window and a door. A door where her energy body or consciousness could fly into the realm and a window where she saw visions, etc. But that morning, it had changed in appearance. The pupil was a vertical, slim oval, housing a red wavy flame and fringed by a lime green light. It resembled the centre of a child's marble or a cat's eye.

The Man on the Throne

December 2nd: In the realm, men walked toward Helena, handing her cards, saying she was a medium and had to start making contact. Then, a king, sitting on a throne wearing a crown, a spotted fur collar, and a jeweled chain across his chest, came drifting towards her. He didn't speak, and we wondered who he was. We hoped that our appointment later that day with a spiritual lady called Maria would shed light on everything, as we were confused. This lady was recommended to us by the Reiki practitioner.

Maria connected with Helena's spirit guides, informing us that Helena was a helper in the spirit world, that her gift would get stronger, and that her spirit guide was on his way. She gave Helena a prayer to say, telling her to make an altar and light a candle over a bowl of water. When the spirits were around, Helena was to say this prayer in the name of Jesus Christ and send the spirits to the Light. The following day, Helena did just that. She closed her eyes and connected with two spirits, Jenny and Margaret. She called them by name and sent them into the Light. She heard other spirits speak, and one said, "I don't want to go," and another said, *"Leave her alone."* It was as if they were in a waiting room, some of whom were reluctant to leave. Later in meditation, Helena asked, "Am I doing my work right? Am I releasing spirits into the Light? She waited and waited and heard a firm voice say, *"Be grateful. Be grateful for the gift that you have been given."* Helena was delighted and called me later, "What do you think of that, Irene? Ha! I can talk to my guides!" Later, she went to the field to feed Belle. She noticed that the air around her had a sparkling component as if a special atmosphere were forming around her, and within this atmosphere floated *two* orbs of light – a second introduction to orbs. The first was in her dream, representing the spirit of the deceased. The second showed their amount increasing.

Guardian Angel Thomas

September 7th & 8th: Helena and I did a Reiki course in Dublin. We thought it would help build her energies, and maybe we might become practitioners in the future. As an exercise, the teacher asked us to connect with our angels and ask intuitively for our angels' names. The other girls asked and picked a name. Helena received the name Thomas, the name of her guardian angel. She had lots of interactions with Thomas, but I have omitted them for brevity.

The Waiting Room

It became Helena's morning routine to bring her children to school, light the candle, and release spirits in the realm; as she released more came, she heard a girl say, *"There are about thirty of us, and not all of us want to go. Some of them are tired."* Helena also heard doors opening and closing as if people were coming in and out of a room.

A Holographic King

December 11th: Helena went travelling within the realm – or rather, her spirit or consciousness went travelling while she sat on the couch in her kitchen. (For the rest of this book, when I refer to Helena's consciousness or spirit travelling, I will say she 'flew' as it is how it felt to her.) In the realm, tunnels of energetic light appeared, and she'd float toward them as if being pulled and guided through to a new place. She learned that the lights in her peripheral vision were angels that flanked her spirit as she travelled. She described herself as 'an energy that flew at great speed through a spaghetti web of swirling, cloudy, pressurized tunnels of light.' Coming to the end of a tunnel, she was spat out and sucked into another, not knowing where she was going but knowing she was being guided. Helena felt she was encouraged to travel further and was learning to navigate new realms. These tunnels of coloured light have been described throughout the centuries by people who have experienced Near-Death Experiences (NDE). This term was coined by Dr. Raymond Moody, based on the knowledge that many people in the initial moments of death commonly recall an experience of floating through a tunnel of light before resuscitation back to life. In one of these tunnels, a woman of light appeared to Helena; she was wearing a full-length period gown. *This was a visual introduction.* Arriving in another realm, Helena became aware of the king's powerful presence. His presence filled Helena's screen with sparkling light. His image wasn't very clear, but she saw his silhouette as she waited for a spirit to arrive. She was told to *"Focus."*

Eventually, a spirit called Francesca came; she was sad and missed her home. Helena comforted her, saying she would send her to the Light and Francesca would love it there. Helena released her. After hours of what Helena thought was an unproductive meditation, she heard a voice say, *"Don't be disappointed."* We didn't know at that time, but this was training for Helena. She was learning how to release spirits to the Light under the guidance of the king.

That afternoon, she went horse riding and felt a pull on her forehead, compelling her to look up. She focused on the clouds, which grew darker, and within them saw smaller clouds that took the form of angel's wings. The sparkling atmosphere surrounded her, and she began to call it 'her twinkles.'

At 5:00 pm, I received a voicemail from Helena; she was excited and said, "I sat blindfolded and asked my angels, "When will I see my spirit guide? How long do I have to wait?" She waited, and then, on the left-side of her screen, she saw a flash of light, then a burst of colour, followed by another flash of light, another burst of colour, and a flash again. It continued for about three minutes. She exclaimed, *"He came, Irene! He came! He came right up in front of me! My whole face was numb with the pressure of him directly in front of me! He was spectacular! A vibrant pink and purple hologram! He sat on his throne as a king, but he didn't speak."*

With the excitement in her voice, I knew Helena had seen something magnificent. She was practically squealing. Helena had called, and the king had come in energetic flashes through the realms. It was like something out of a sci-fi movie. It certainly made my journey home from work a lot more enjoyable.

Two Thrones

December 12th: Helena entered the realm, where *two* spirit guides seated on thrones waited for her. On one sat a king, and on the other, a woman. Her throne was slightly different than his, as he had a headrest while hers did not. She wore a long gown like the woman before. Large angels with wings so long that they were sitting on the earth were present. They spoke to Helena, and she remembered hearing things like, *'You will be doing spiritual work, and we are Catholics.'* The hymn 'Jesus Loves Me' was played for her. They showed her a hand and a pen, indicating she should write things down.

A Knight

December 13th: Helena stood in the field looking skywards when a circle of energy (aura) appeared; within it was an angel. There was also an outline of her guide sitting on his throne. She continued to observe, and he turned around in his aura to let her have a good look at him. Helena knelt, prayed, and thanked them for showing themselves. She said, *"Irene, if anyone had seen me, they would have thought I was mad."*

The field where her horse was stabled is down a small lane, a dead-end stopped by dunes to the beach. I visualized her kneeling on the ground, praying. If what Helena was telling me was true, and I had no reason to doubt her, she was talking about heavenly visitations like Our Lady in Lourdes. I knew something was coming but didn't know what. Later, while meditating, she had a vision of a knight on horseback carrying a shield – *this was another visual introduction.* That night, she felt negative energy surround her, and its effects made her feel low, making her cry.

Jesus and Knights in Battle

December 14th: Helena woke to a vision of Jesus wearing a crown of thorns. This was followed by a vision of knights in full amour riding into battle. She simultaneously felt the negative energy from the night before. Later that day, Helena went into the realm, where approximately fifteen spirit guides waited for her: the wolf, the woman in the big dress, the king, who now had steps leading up to his throne as if it were on a pedestal and a circle of light behind him. There were more, but she couldn't make them out as their body outlines were blurred within the colored lights of their spirits. But she saw a knight wearing a chained glove holding his sword in the air. Helena said, "They are all showing themselves to me."

In hindsight, I believe the knights riding into battle, along with the negative energy Helena felt, was their way of showing her that this was going to be a fight for the Light against the darkness for Jesus. She was made to feel the sadness that came with it – maybe that was how Jesus was feeling. But at that time, we didn't know what was happening.

Outside, You Will See

December 23rd: Helena went into the realm to ask questions.

Helena: Has my eye changed?

Guides: Yes, you will be angry and confused.

Helena: Do I still have to release spirits to the Light as part of my work?

Guides: Yes. Outside, you will see.

She wondered if she might see a ghost. She didn't want to. She was terrified of seeing them.

A Native American & Grids

December 28th: Helena was in the realm, flying through three lime-green grids. Passing through one, a Native American man showed himself; this was another *visual introduction.* (She would channel him later, but I have omitted it.) She was told to "go through" and travelled into people's homes. She viewed our niece Sonya in her own kitchen, fields, birds eating food on the ground, and lots of everyday things, as if her mind could travel anywhere, like 'remote viewing.' She heard the words, '*Getting stronger.*'

King Luther

December 29th: In the realm, Helena released a boy and was waiting for another spirit when her body began to shake. Her spirit guide came floating in front of her. He introduced himself as Luther. They spoke telepathically, but he had an energetic pull on her each time he spoke. So, when he spoke, Helena's head was moved forward by his energy as if she were bowing. That day, Helena saw the 'heatwave energy' at the bottom of her bed, describing it as "Moving particles of gaseous energy in the air" or "a special type of atmosphere." She believed she was beginning to see spirits outside and didn't mind seeing energy or orbs, but not ghosts.

Angels, Orbs & Yvonne Beauvais

Field of Angels

December 30th: Helena was in the field and sent me a voicemail. She was excited. "Irene, I'm looking up at the sky, and there are about sixteen oval-shaped energy bubbles in a semicircle bobbing around me. In the bubbles are angels, and I can see the outline of their heads and wings. They were emitting a green electrical spark that drew my attention to them. Then I got a feeling of someone behind me, and I asked, angel Thomas, is that you? And I was pulled backward. I asked, are Raphael and Michael standing on either side of me? And I started to sway from right to left. Irene, I don't know whether to laugh or cry, but angels surround me."

Sr. Yvonne Beauvais

December 31st: Helena bought a deck of angel cards as previously advised by Maria and pulled a card from the deck with the title Archangel Michael. Suddenly, she felt her body being pulled to the left, and then the voice of Archangel Michael spoke to her, *"Have faith in what's happening; it's meant to be."*

Then, closing her eyes, she connected with Luther, who spoke about her future. During this seemingly innocuous conversation, Luther, like a diplomat, began slowly guiding the conversation to what he really wanted to talk about.

Luther: *We have known each other before. You are the reincarnated soul of Sr. Yvonne Beauvais. She lives again in you. She is in your soul.*

Helena: *Who's Yvonne Beauvais?*

Helena jumped onto Google and found some information about Yvonne, but most of it was in French. Helena sent me a photo of Sr.

Yvonne - she existed! This is a little of what we learned about this incredible nun.

Yvonne Beauvais was born on July 16, 1901. At the age of eleven, Yvonne offered herself to Jesus, writing in what appeared to be her own blood, "O my little Jesus, I give myself to Thee completely and forever. I shall always want what Thou shalt want. I shall do all that Thou shalt tell me to do. I shall live for Thee, I shall live in silence, and if it be Thy will, I shall suffer much in silence. I beg Thee to make me become a very great saint, a martyr. Make me always faithful. **I want to save many souls** and love thee more than everyone else, but I also want to be very little to give Thee more glory. I want to possess Thee, my little Jesus, and to shine with Thee. I want to belong to Thee alone, but above all, I want Thy will."

In 1922, Jesus appeared to Yvonne in a monastery in Brittany. She later became an Augustinian nun and took the name Mother Yvonne-Aimee of Jesus. She helped allied soldiers and French resistance fighters during World War II, and in 1946, she established the Federation of the Augustinian monasteries. Sr. Yvonne died of a brain hemorrhage on February 3rd, 1951.

We stared in shock at Yvonne's photo. Helena loved that for Sr. Yvonne to save the soldiers' lives; she dressed them up as nuns! Sr. Yvonne was extremely courageous. As she looked at the photo, Helena asked Luther, "Was that me?" Her head was pulled to her chest. This was Luther's way of saying a definite yes! Helena and I were stunned.

The Year 2020

God, His Army & Hierarchy

Loving Beings of Light

January 2nd: Helena asked Luther if he would speak to me, and he agreed. A dream of mine was about to come true. I would question a spiritual being about the meaning of life. Over the following weeks, there were many channels from Luther. (I have only included parts of these.) The next day, I went to Helena's cottage and made tea while Helena, masked, sat on the couch. Luther connected, and Helena channeled his words. Firstly, I thanked Luther for talking with me. Helena's head was thrown forward, and I knew Luther was about to come through. I started asking lighthearted questions. He answered politely and even made a joke. When I asked who I was in a previous life? Luther replied, 'Jennifer Saunders.' Helena laughed, "What, Luther? Are you making a joke?" She asked. We both laughed. I have often been told that I have the mannerisms of the English Comedienne Jennifer Saunders, and I love her comedy. So, we both got the joke. When I started asking serious questions, the information from Luther flowed quickly, more fluidly, and over time in rhyme. You will see its format as the book goes on. Sorry if I'm not explaining it correctly.

Irene: *What are we here to learn?*

Luther: *Compassion, gratitude, love, values, lots of values, understanding, unity and forgiveness.*

Irene: *If we learn lessons, why do we have to keep coming back? And how are we judged? By our faith or by our actions?*

Helena: *I can hear music. The song is* Do You Want to Live Forever *by* Queen.

Luther: *To live forever!*

   Do not be misunderstood why we are here,

we learn and grow; we truly live forever within this world,

peace and happiness will be yours,

we are all as one; we continue to learn and grow.

That is what we are: loving beings of light.

Light is within you always.

This you will learn and know,

You are always in our hearts.

What we do is what we become,

if you are true of heart, you will succeed.

If you are patient, loving, and kind, you will become one with Him.

If not, you go nowhere, an endless depth where there is no compassion or love, only misery and sadness.

For there will be endless, you go no further, you're trapped and stuck.

Use the kindness in your hearts to help them succeed.

Yes, we are judged by our actions.

What will be, will be.

Irene: *If God truly loves us, how can he send us to that endless place?*

Luther: *They're not for God; they are not like ye angels of God.*

They are blind; they cannot see what true love is for eternity.

We have tried and tried and tried again, but still, they cannot see;

the true love you need to live for eternity.

They have fallen, and they can't come back,

the darkness is where they stay and where they shall be;

there is no light within them, like you and me.

Things will happen. He will try again and again;

no matter what He does, they still want to sin.

Take time to understand He,

true love forever, and forever He will be.

Jesus loves us all, but these people they cannot see.

There is no light for them; darkness, they will fall;

There is no getting out of there- no getting out at all.

They will; they will, they will,

they will fall.

We took a tea break, but Luther came through again.

Luther:

> *I love you both, and you both love me.*
>
> *You will live forever and will be so happy*
>
> *For you love Him, and He loves ye.*
>
> *God does love, and God does care,*
>
> *We truly love you; you have heard our call*
>
> *You will do your best, great or small.*
>
> End of channel.

Speaking with Luther felt like being wrapped in the arms of a loving friend; we were spellbound listening to him. He said, "You have heard our call. You will do your best, great or small." We didn't know what he wanted us to do, but he made us feel secure by convincing us of God's love for us. I believe this was to prepare us for what was to come. It would also help us endure what would follow. We really miss Luther.

Our Destiny

January 6th: While releasing spirits under Luther's guidance, he explained that he was to come to Helena when she was eighteen, but she wasn't ready. She recorded her meditation, and when listening to the audio, she can be heard inhaling long, deep breaths as if in a trance. There were silences as she listened to Luther, and when she thought she'd heard him correctly, she repeated his words for the recording. She whispered, "Any information for me today, Luther?"

Luther answered seven minutes later.

Luther: *I am a messenger from Him to help you go on upon your spiritual journey.*

It will all unfold the way it's supposed to; divine timing is what it is; it is our destiny.

For He has made eternity for everyone, and with the light inside them, this will be.

We will give you the power within, and from this day forth, you will never sin.

These are His gifts from me to you, and these gifts you shall never abuse.

As they are pure from within the light, forever, they are yours; we have given you this sight.

So, don't be foolish and abuse it in any way; these are your gifts, and they have been given to you with love.

Be true, be kind, be caring, and be proud. The love within you will outshine the rest.

You have beaming love coming from your chest. The sparkle of light is within your eyes.

You are the most beautiful person inside.

Yvonne, you know this: Yvonne is within you; you were a saint. This is true.

A beautiful soul, and that soul is within you - the cheekiness, the fun, and her laughter, too, is all within you, from this time and after.

Really understand how special you are for He, Helena; you are special, as special as can be.

You will sense and know this in your heart. The very best of luck to you and Irene.

What He puts together will never part. You and Irene are very special within his heart.

Please relate this message to her. You are special; this is for sure.

End of channel.

Then I heard Helena speaking once again with Luther.

Helena*: I will begin to sense more spirits approaching me? And I could experience this at any time of day? "Oh Luther, how brilliant,"* she remarked cynically.

Luther: *There won't be many in a day. One, two, three at the most. You will have to know your prayers to release them. Learn your prayers now; you will see the power that is within you; you need to set them free.*

It will go on for a few months more, then you will be free from doing this, I am sure. End of channel.

Then Came the Orbs

January 8th: Helena felt a tug on her forehead that summoned her to work as about seventeen lime-green orbs drifted through her home. Helena was annoyed because she wanted to go horse riding and told them cheekily to wait until she got back. Riding her horse, she saw more orbs and said her prayer to see what would happen. Sparks of light flitted around in the atmosphere. She asked Luther, "Am I releasing spirits?"

Luther: *Yes.*

Helena: *Are the sparks of light angels?*

Luther: *Yes.*

She voice-mailed, *"Irene, I can release while I am out."* It had taken us a while to comprehend that Helena was working for God. Why her? Every day, we were in disbelief, and our most common statement was, *"This is mad, just mad."* We wondered what else could happen. There couldn't be much more. We were so very wrong. This was only the beginning. What was to come was beyond imagination. That evening, Helena prayed constantly because her house was full of orbs. She asked them to leave, but they didn't. She asked me, *"What should I do, Irene? I have prayed a lot, but there are still more. I don't get it … I'm so confused."*

Angels Collect Spirits

January 9th: Helena was in the field, surrounded by her 'twinkles.' Feeling wonderfully special, she voice-mailed, saying, *"They surround me, Irene; you know the usual,"* she giggled. When she got home, she voice-mailed again, this time exasperated, "Irene, the house is full of orbs. Luther said it would be two or three; he must have meant two or three hundred! I'm going to start praying again. She said, "I have released roughly forty-three," in a voicemail. Luther promised me that's it for today. There were so many. I asked Yvonne to help me, and Irene, I started to recite the prayer very fast, like those guys who sell the cattle in the cattle market. The prayer was flying out of my mouth! I was so tired, and they just kept coming. Irene, when I close my eyes, I go into the realm and see pink in the distance; that's Luther. Today, as I said my prayers, I felt pressure on the left-hand side of my head. I could see the spirits come into the realm from the left-hand side. From the right-hand side, I saw pink lights meet them in the middle and shoot upwards. This happened repeatedly as I prayed. I asked Luther if there were any more to release when I was done because there was a calm. Then, four angels flew up and hovered in front of me in the realm. I could clearly see their heads and wings, Irene; they were so beautiful." (I could hear the joy in Helena's voice.) Irene, as I prayed, I saw the angels collect the spirits, and they zoomed off together. It was unbelievable. "So now we know that when our spirits make it to this realm, they are met with angels."

The Presence in the Cloud of Light

January 10th: Helena rode her horse among the twinkles, explaining over voicemail that she had a weird feeling in her stomach and the pull on her head was strong. She looked at the clouds and saw a vision of a king seated on a throne, his hands folded on his lap. She untacked her horse and sat on a wooden bench beside the stable. A hymn was playing in her head,

He is Lord, He is lord, He is risen from the dead, and He is Lord,

every knee shall bow every tongue confess, that Jesus Christ is Lord.

It was a bright morning, and the sun beamed down as she closed her eyes. She felt she was being made to bow, so she bowed, then felt she should recite the Lord's Prayer, and so began. She noticed an unusual type of cloud and had difficulty describing it. She bowed again, and the cloud of mist infused with white light enveloped her. Even though the sun shone, she was cold and thought God would speak to her. She sat in this mist for around twenty minutes until her phone alarm alerted her to collect her son. She said it was very strange: "No words were uttered, but I sensed a presence, saw a light, and felt compelled to bow and say the Our Father." She left and went home for tea to warm herself up because she was so cold.

Later that evening, in a mass for her son's upcoming First Holy Communion she felt a strong pull on her forehead. As she looked around, orbs were everywhere. She was compelled to pray, so she released as much as she could while thinking it was weird that spirits were stuck in a church. The next day, she asked Luther why spirits were stuck in a church.

Luther: *A church is only a place of God, you know;*

spirits get stuck, and they need to go.

You just release as many as you can.

Helena: *Why are people like me channeling spirit? Are there more people than me?*

Luther: *Yes, there are a few earth angels there, too; they release, release for He.*

This is work that just needs to be done. Helena, you are not the only one.

This work needs to be done. They all have to go through the process to learn and grow.

What you plant, you grow. You sow the seeds, you water lots, sit back and watch them grow.

This all has to be done.

Spirits of Light

January 13th: Helena asked if she could come to my house for tea. Luther interrupted and said enthusiastically, "Yes, let's go." I said, "Well, if Luther wants to come for tea, he is very welcome." When

Helena arrived, I made a pot of tea and took out my phone for recording. The previous day, Luther had a gift for Helena. Our deceased mother had come through and talked to us. She told her that she was so proud of us and the work we would do. It turned out Luther had a gift for me, too. In the middle of a channel, Helena stopped and said, Finola? Finola? Is that you? She heard her actual voice. Finola was my best friend, who died just before this all began on August 30th, 2019. She was a loving, gentle, but very fearful person. I was worried about this. In her long message, she said, *"I'm not afraid anymore. Irene, I'm not afraid. It's all gone. They take it away."* It was *exactly* what I needed to hear. I thanked Luther for his wonderful gift to me. It was all so unreal.

After hearing Finola's message, we discussed what she might be like in the afterlife. Luther jumped back in and talked about the afterlife.

Luther: *She is a spirit of light that shines so bright.*

Irene, that's all you are, you know, micro, micro.

Everyone has a job or at least has work assigned to them that they must complete.

Up here there, there is lots of work that has to be done, too.

Comforting other souls that also come through.

Children and babies have to be taken care of, too.

Everyone is different, you see; it's just like you and me.

They also learn and grow.

The work is endless up here, you see; there are so many of you.

There are processes everyone needs to go through.

Pain and hurt have to be taken away.

Bring them back to being pure once more.

You can get reincarnated in lots of different ways.

There is a selection of each process that they go through.

Who are they going to be next? Are they going to be a doctor? Are they going to be a vet?

Or are they going to come down as an animal, a bird, or a fly?

It's all energy around you; it goes on and on, it's endless.

Lots of work, lots of things to do, and Helena, we will be feeding loads through to you.

Spiritual paths they all have to meet.

Everyone goes on a journey, and it goes on, and it goes on, and it goes on.

Learn, and learn, and learn, and learn again. Different aspects of life.

We go on, and we go on, and we go on lots more.

End of channel.

Helena described channelling Luther as 'a lovely warm feeling of love', or 'a flow of calm and peaceful energy.' Helena left my house and went to feed Belle before collecting the kids from school. I received a voicemail rather quickly; she was excited! "Irene, it's happened again. I was in the presence of Jesus. The sun was shining, and I closed my eyes, looked up, and saw light-infused clouds falling. Luther said, *"Here He comes. He is coming to see you."* And then the light came soaring down closer and closer to me. Then, it became much colder; I was freezing. The mist and the clouds were on my face again. He was there in the light, and I could hear the hymn, "Jesus Loves Me." Then the light changed to a kind of moonlight, and I just knelt there on my hunkers and looked at the light, and He said, (Helena's phone had been turned off, but His words went something like this), *"My child of Grace. You are going to spread the love and light. I am the creator of all things: the wind, the sun, the birds, the trees, and the air that you breathe. I love you, my child, I love you."*

Kings and their Armies

Helena drove to the field that evening, bringing her son James and dog Hank for company. She was nervous, believing she might see something appear, and she did - an orb. She began praying, hoping it would go away, but another followed her into the stable. Afraid, she jumped into her car and drove home, noticing that orbs were everywhere along the road. Pulling into her garden, two came floating in behind her. One was so big she thought it was going to manifest into someone. She voice-mailed, "Irene, there is now a queue of orbs lining up outside the back door. I have a lot of releasing to do tonight. OMG!"

Helena prayed all night while watching angels in the realm collect spirits and whip them upwards towards Luther and into the Light. That night, she saw *more* kings seated on thrones. Then, in the middle of her screen, she saw a line of armoured soldiers with headgear, spears, and swords. They walked straight up to her, then veered off to the right. She continued to watch this, saying she could *feel* them. The soldiers were presenting themselves to her. The visions of kings and soldiers were *visual introductions* - something new was beginning.

Foot Soldiers of Heaven

January 14th: Luther explained to Helena, "Jesus just wanted to tell you that He loved you." She asked if the orbs were going to turn into human form; he said no, but she would be seeing more. He agreed with her suggestion that from now on, the spirits could be released in groups of four, as it took up much of her day. Helena asked about the soldiers, and he said, *'They are the foot soldiers of heaven. You are at the gateway of heaven when you see all of us."* Then something funny happened that made us giggle. As Helena prayed, the orbs floated over to the water, shrunk, and disappeared. Helena moved the bowl from her coffee table into a little box shelving unit. As she called the spirits to enter in fours, she heard a woman say something like, "Wow, it's hard to squish in here." Four Orbs was a bit of a tight squeeze, apparently. Helena put her hand under an orb to see what would happen, but it floated away like a bubble. The orbs were everywhere.

Evolved Spirits

January 16th: Helena woke to see the image of three people very clearly - The Native American, Luther, and Jesus wearing a crown of thorns. In a channel with Luther, Helena asked a few questions.

Helena: *Luther, are you a king?*

Luther: *Yes, I am a king for He; yes, you did see me.*

Helena: *I had a straight neck, and someone initially fixed it. Who was it? God or Jesus?*

Luther: *Our Lord. Our Creator. He.*

Helena: *Why me? And why do I see all these kings and queens on thrones?*

Luther: *You're special, Helena; this is true; you've evolved spirits in your soul; you have more than two. Twenty-four spirits in your soul.*

Christianity, you see, they all work for He, including me; this is meant to be.

This is how you will spread the word of Christ; it's just going to happen overnight.

We have been displaying ourselves to you for a long time.

The top hierarchy spokesman is me; I'll be introducing them all to ye.

End of channel

We tried to absorb what Luther told us: Helena had twenty-four spirits in her soul. We didn't understand what any of this meant.

The Hierarchy

January 17th: Helena came to my house, and we lit the fire and made tea. In retrospect, this was a lovely time for us both. We sat on the sofa, and Helena put on her eye mask while I hit record on my phone. When she closed her eyes, the spirits were ready and waiting for her in the realm. Helena described what she was witnessing for the recording.

Helena: I see a swirling-colored cloudy tunnel, and I am flying through. The angels are guiding me somewhere. I feel like I am being pulled slowly, like a fisherman reeling in a fish. The colors twist around in a swirling mist - blue, pink, and burgundy and within the mist of colors, I see a woman sitting on a throne wearing a long dress.

I noticed Helena rocking from side to side as if she were bobbing in a boat; she felt a burning sensation at the back of her head. Helena asked the lady her name, and the lady responded - *"Elizabeth I!"* Helena told her she was pretty and *I couldn't believe my ears!*

Helena: *What do you want to say to us today?*

Elizabeth I: *Hi Helena, what I say is true time and time again;*

       the planet you're on, it will be at an end.

This scared me, and without missing a beat, as if reading my mind or my mind was one with hers, Elizabeth said, *"I don't want to scare you, Irene, but it is true.*

You are our angels on earth, and we will come through you.

The light and the darkness are going to meet again."

Helena: *Irene, I see a blue flashing light, and a big, burly man is within it. He's a big! Big guy! He is wearing armor, and he is sitting on a throne.*

Henry VIII: *Henry VIII, this is true; I am inside of you.*

I pray, I pray, I pray, he has something to say.

I'm here, and I have never gone away.

I still rule from above here.

We still all work for He, you see.

We are all still here, still here within the Light.

The world is in trouble; we need to change our way, or it will be gone!

We are all here, but we are all trying to stay strong.

Can you not see what ye are doing? It's just unreal.

There are a few of you that are trying to change their ways,

We can feel the love from inside their hearts.

We need all to do more to save this planet; this is for sure.

We need to share the love and the light for them to have sight.

Destroying the world bit by bit, we have to keep going; we cannot quit.

The planet will be no more, will be no more, will be no more,

Keep going the way you are that is for sure.

We are coming to share the Word of Our Lord.

He is going to call out to all of ye.

Elizabeth I: *Oh, Helena, will you behave?*

Helena: *Sorry, but you are bashing my head like it's a basketball.*

There was such a strong pull from the hierarchy's energy that it tugged on Helena's head and hurt her. Elizabeth told her to behave and keep quiet so she could keep the connection.

Another man zoomed toward Helena; his spirit was full of fiery energy. Helena flexed her arm to show me that this man was a fighter!

Helena: *Irene, you'd want to feel the energy of this spirit! I can feel the power in him! This guy looks like he has a stick or a sword in his hand.*

Helena then asked this man to clarify who he was.

Helena: *Henry? King Henry again?*

Then the man clarified: *"King Henry V."*

Henry V shouted the following with a lot of fiery energy.

Henry V: *Yes! This is he! We are also inside of ye! We are all hierarchical!*

We are here to spread the word, for He is not happy at all.

The people of the planet need to hear our call.

Little by little, they are tearing it apart. We're coming to tell you now; we have to make a start. Change the ways it has to be.

Unbelievable damage you are doing to ye.

You need to snap out of it; it needs to happen now!

We are here to help you, and we are here to show you how.

They are all going to have to hear His call.

There is a warrior coming through; he wants to speak to you.

Warrior of Light: *Helena, they will hear our call; we have our horses here and all.*

Fight there will be; we will fight for He. The darkness hasn't got a chance against He.

We won before, and we will again; the only thing is the matter of when.

Helena, it will, it will, it will happen soon. We will always fight, and we will never stop.

The darkness will be doomed, and doomed it will be, but they will never beat He.

You have to listen to He, or ye won't be.

Helena*: Irene, the colour is changing, and they are all coming out of a tunnel. There is an image of Jesus on the cross.*

I looked at Helena and was surprised to see that her arms were open wide, palms turned upwards like a priest saying mass. She felt herself being pushed back. "Whoa!" Helena cried out unexpectedly, and her head was thrown forward like she was going downhill on a rollercoaster. I watched in astonishment. She said she was flying very fast down a purple tunnel, and as her spirit flew, her body went with the turns as if she were rounding sharp bends on a motorbike. She was stopped and made to wait, then someone met her and pulled her forward. She felt herself climbing higher and higher, going somewhere different, travelling through smoky green, pink, and purple clouds.

Helena: *Where are they taking me to?*

Guide: *It takes a little while this time.*

I watched Helena lean forward as she described being pulled down once again through misty purple and blue tunnels. Helena's head turned right (still blindfolded) as she was guided in a different direction. She reached another realm where more spirits paraded themselves - a woman wearing a wide dress with puffy shoulders rose from a throne and walked regally toward Helena - her spirit was shimmering. There were several men; one sat on a throne in a changing cloud of misty colors, another wore a red and blue sash, others had puffed out collars, while some wore cloaks with chains across their chests – some had a train. There were maidens wearing dresses with puffy sleeves with scarves draping over their arms. Like Queen Elizabeth I, a woman with a fanned-out collar presented herself and bowed. Warriors of Light were marching. For whatever reason, maybe it was to show order or to not overwhelm Helena, but everyone Helena met had to be introduced. This was another visual introduction that included the Hierarchy and Warriors of Light. The parade continued until Helena left to collect her son Christopher from school. Arriving home, Helena felt a pull on her forehead and saw a large angel with a human body form and large wings hovering in the sky. She voice-mailed from her car, saying they were drawing her attention to something in the sky but couldn't make out what it was. A few minutes later, I heard her again, "Irene, they have been pulling and nodding my head, and I looked up to the sky, and I can see it clearly now; it's a crucifix!" The misty clouds had formed the shape of a crucifix. That evening, Helena was tired, and her house was full of orbs. She voice-mailed saying, "I want to relax Irene, but the prayer is in my head. I know I must keep working because my mind is not my own anymore. It's taken over my life."

The Army of Light

January 18th: It was morning, and more spirits introduced themselves in the realm.

Catherine The Great: *We come today to tell you that all we say is true.*

It's time to share the Word of God.

We will do what we can to help you all,

there are so many humans who can't help but fall

to their knees from the darkness within; they can't help but sin.

We have the Army of Light inside you,

we are going to help this planet from inside you.

We work for He; this is true, this is the start, we are all there to play our part.

Right and wrong, there will be a storm.

A storm, from the heavens, you will see; this will be.

Then Helena saw an incredibly beautiful Knight on horseback. He called himself a *Knight of the Light.*

Knight of The Light: *Knight of the Light, I'm here to fight,*

there are so many of us, you see; we all work for He;

ready to guard the Gates of the Great.

Later that evening, Luther said he was letting the hierarchy come through bit by bit as there were so many. Helena said she could *feel* their personalities and would mimic their tone as she spoke. She was watching a movie and eating chips when she felt a pull on her forehead. Closing her eyes, a woman wearing a long flowing dress with material draped over her arm stood there. Helena was shocked at how quickly the woman appeared and felt she was being summoned. Having not finished her chips, she voice-mailed, asking, "Irene, is this going to happen all the time? Can I not even watch a bit of TV in the evening? I have to go." She hit record and spoke to them, but she was very annoyed. Some of the people who introduced themselves were Catherine of Aragon (who has a beautiful personality), Catherine of Valois, Edward the Great, a very grand lady who said she was Henry VIII's aunt Patricia, Prince Oliver,

Queen Martha, King George III and a Joseph White who said he was Henry the VIII's bookkeeper. They advised her once again to document their names. Then Luther concluded the evening's introductions by saying,

Luther: *Get some sleep; I know you have other things to do.*

King Luther the Third! I'm at the top of the hierarchy.

I'm leaving you now, for sure, but tomorrow, I will be introducing you to more.

Then you will get to sit with us all; you will be here with us, standing so proud and tall; and from here, you will never fall; you are his children of Grace.

King Luther

January 19th: Helena sat puffing on her Vape while Hank snored gently beside her. It only dawned on her then that she never asked Luther who He was. His answer shocked both of us.

Helena: *King Luther, what is your full name? You are Martin Luther King?!! ...No! I didn't know who you were! 1953 died at 62? 52? Activist for people's rights? That is what you are known for.*

Luther made a joke, which Helena repeated.

Helena: *You're a people person, you know,*

even back then, that long ago. Diplomat for the people?

For people's rights? That's what you were known for?"

We are once again in awe. God made Martin Luther King a king! So, it is true – we are judged by our actions.

King Solomon's Army

January 25th: Helena sat blindfolded beside me in my living room. It was a frosty day, and we lit the fire and made tea. She viewed the parade of spirits once again. Their spirit lights flashed quickly. *"We are trying to let you see us clearly today,"* said the woman in a dress with puffy shoulders whom we had learned was Catherine the Great.

Hierarchy: *We will come through when we are ready to come through.*

Helena: *Oh God, Irene, there is a big queue on the left-hand side. They are showing me the length of the queue. It goes on and on. I see their heads mainly…. it is an army. OMG! I see a king! He is wearing a lot of heavy material and a chain around his neck!*

This particular king made an impression on Helena as she was astonished when she saw him. So, over to the left of the line, in vision, there were rows of armies: soldiers, knights, warriors, and kings among them. Then she heard, "King Solomon's Army." Helena's head was pulled forward, meaning she was correct.

Catherine The Great: *The end of the world is coming for ye, and we're here to work it out.*

There has been no one like you, Helena, before; you have opened this door.

Door to the hierarchy, you see, it's incredible, you see,

once more we will get to play our part through ye.

You will stand with us to win this fight; it's there; it's nearly in sight.

We will fight once more, you see, but we will all be fighting for He.

For He is the creator of all, and we have heard His call.

Rounded us all up one by one to get the job done.

We are all here with our peers; you see, we are in the best of company.

King, Queen, and Knight of the Light, to be precise,

I would never have thought this would be possible to do.

Likeminded people, all of us, you know,

worrying about the world and what way it's going to go.

You are conversing with me, you see; the voice you hear is always me.

I'm the one who spoke to you when you slept.

Okay, we must part, but we will be a work of art.

Helena: *I want to take a break.*

Catherine the Great: *What may.*

We had our tea break, and when Helena put on her blindfold, she was led straight into a tunnel by Catherine the Great.

Catherine the Great: *You are the only one on earth who has even been here before.*

Follow me, and I will show you the right way to go. What an amazing journey He is taking you on. Keep up! We are nearly there, my dear.

It is quite profound about how far you have been able to come.

We need to go through here, can you see?

This is the door we needed to come for.

Come along; you can walk in with me.

Quite long corridors, you see.

Helena walked through a corridor where rows of soldiers were walking.

Catherine The Great: *Armies of all the kings, you see?*

They are all showing themselves to ye.

They display themselves more and more, just to make sure you see.

King Solomon: *King Solomon. Hello, my dear. We become stronger and stronger up here, you know. We are all getting prepared, you know.*

Helena was shown very beautiful black and white horses. A man on horseback came right up in front of her.

Horseman: *We are dressed in our finest and our best.*

Helena: There are three horsemen in front of me now. Another soldier on a black horse has frills and stuff. He's bowing to me, and I'm bowing back. They are showing themselves in all their glory and attire.

Horseman: *We will talk to you soon, my dear,*

we are just parading ourselves for you to see;

it's an honor, really.

You are up here with the best!

Armor, shields, and horses and all; we are letting you see it all.

They turned to the right, then left, and to the front with their swords.

Horseman: *What do you think, Helena? Don't we all look great?*

Helena: *Yes, you all look fantastic!*

King Solomon: *There are so many of us it's hard to get your head around.*

Yes, that's the end of our queue; it just goes on and on.

In numbers, we are strong; we will overcome the darkness you see.

We fight to exist, and this will be a war that is not to be missed!

For you have the sight, Helena, so we are allowing you to see.

We are all here to fight for He; we fight to exist for eternity.

For the world will end, and it will be no more;

you all need to change your ways, that is for sure.

We will all come and fight with light, strength, and power.

We will overcome the rest; it will be like playing a game of chess.

We will soar like the wind, you see,

We will all sacrifice ourselves for He.

The soldiers began to chant:

Here here, what may, here we are going to stay.

Here here, what may, here we are going to stay.

The troops are here to fight another day.

Here here, what may we are going here to stay.

Angels: *We are going somewhere where no one has ever gone before.*

Then Helena went flying again through green and red tunnels. She felt she was travelling a good distance, and even though she sat on my couch, she looked like she was on a roller coaster, one minute leaning forward, travelling downwards, then pulling back sharply going upwards. This lasted around five minutes; then, her brow furrowed as she tried to focus on the new guides who greeted her.

Guides: *We have brought you here today to let you see,*

how far away you have to travel to be with He.

This is the place of dreams, you see.

No one like you has ever been here before.

We are relying on you for what you have to do for us,

it's so important the earth can combust!

With honor and Grace, you will proceed.

Helena was led away again. This time travelling swiftly. I watched her hands shake violently like they were conducting energy.

Helena: *Irene, I'm soaring over clouds now and have slowed down. Someone is walking toward me with an orange light. He is saying, "Yes, it is He. Jesus Christ."*

Jesus Christ: *Yes, it is He. You are speaking to me.*

I have been waiting for you to come to me.

Helena began to cry.

Jesus Christ: *Don't cry, my child, I love ye.*

Can you feel my arms around you?

Welcome, my child; you have travelled so far,

to be here in the presence of me.

The world is not in a great place;

it needs us all to fight with grace.

My child, you are very important to us all,

it's really nice to meet you without having to fall.

The gifts I give to you, you must follow them all through.

The power and strength you have is all within you.

We have given you everything you need to succeed.

You will help us win this fight for all.

End of message.

Helena: *Irene, His light is right up there.*

Blindfolded, Helena pointed to the ceiling. Her head was right back on the couch, looking straight up at the ceiling; her arms were open wide like a priest saying mass. Helena and I were once again in shock.

God Leads His Armies

God & The Flow

January 21st: Helena was seeing less of Luther - Catherine the Great had taken over. In visions, Helena was shown endless rows of armies on horseback, leaving and marching through what she described as 'a hot, dusty land,' where the villages didn't look too different from the sand around them. Helena described what she was seeing.

Helena: *They are marching through a long, very, very narrow canyon. There's not much room on either side of them for their horses to go through.*

The soldiers, dressed in their finery, were leaving their land and starting their journey for the fight. Where they were going? Or where they were coming from? We didn't know. And we didn't know what it was all about. Later, Helena meditated and was met by a person who called herself Kitty.

Kitty: *All the army are after going on.*

They're all moving for the fight, for the fight of the Light.

You're going on an incredible journey for He.

You are so tired, there is a lot going on,

but my sweet, you're going to have to be strong.

This will take a lot out of you.

That is why you are feeling so tired and drained, you see.

It's all the preparation that is getting ready for He.

You must never fall from temptation from the dark.

Don't get tempted; he will always try this, you see.

Try to pull you in the wrong direction, the wrong direction away from He.

Then, a Knight of the Light came to guide Helena through tunnels.

Knight of the Light: *Come on now, follow me.*

Helena*: Where are we going now?*

Knight of the Light: *Wait until you see.*

Warrior of Light: *Hi Helena, I am a Warrior of the Light. Are you alright?*

Follow me. We are all in a circle, you see.

Helena viewed horses flying around in a whirlwind.

Warrior of Light: *Flying around like the wind. Can you see?*

Helena: *I can see.*

Warrior of Light: *This is the Army of the Light.*

We are working now, day and night.

We are all going to embark on our journey soon.

We are ready to take on the dark.

Helena: *Really?*

Knight of the Light: *Look here, Helena, it's time now; we need to go.*

The Knight of the Light guided Helena to another place. Then, a powerful, commanding male voice came through. You *knew* you had to listen to Him - you were *made* to listen. It was God. As He spoke, His voice continued to rise - with that, Helena's did also.

GOD: *I Am the Mighty One that is talking to you now.*

Creator of this world, this is me.

And I have put it all there for the world to see.

This is my job for Ye, that you will have to do.

For the Light will win, we will succeed again.

The darkness will never overcome me

wait, Irene and Helena, you will see;

for you are the chosen ones for me.

You will do everything you are told you have to do.

You will follow through for me, what I have planned for thee.

This is a contract that you have already signed for me.

You can't not remember this contract! You had signed it before you came down!

Now is the time for you to fulfill it! (STERN)

The time is now!

I am the Lord, the Lord of the above.

I stand where I stood before.

This is the Word of God!

You will do all I say, and you will do no more.

The mighty one I am, and the mighty one I will stay.

I am the creator of this earth in every way.

Everyone will do what I say. This is the way that it has to go.

The planet needs to change, and the time is now!

This world will evaporate and explode; it will be no more.

I will leave you now, but know this once more.

I am He, creator of all, and without me, there is no life,

no light, no rain, no sea, no air; it will all disappear.

It won't be created again!

The world needs to stand up and look after it now!

Helena and Irene, we will help you show them how.

DO YOUR WORK!

Helena: *HOLY SHIT!*

Helena felt her jaw opening and heard a voice say,

"Don't scream or don't shout; just open your mouth.

The power of He is going within side ye."

As Helena's jaw was forced open, she saw visions of the universe: stars, planets, solar systems, and galaxies - they flashed in front of her. (At the time, I didn't understand these flashes of the universe – but what is God? Is He not everything?) As Helena continued to lie there, she voice-mailed, *"Irene, I see the Army of Light; the soldiers are marching towards my head, then evaporate in front of me - as if they are going into me. You would think my third eye is a portal from the spirit world through me to the earth plane."* It was as if Helena could see everything that was happening in the spirit world. She lay on her bed and let them march through. This process of letting the armies march through, which continued over the following weeks, became what we called The Flow, and The Flow was *very* important to God. We really had no idea what was going on. This is exactly what happened, but it is beyond our understanding.

That evening, Helena walked her dogs and was followed by two orbs, and more were joining, so she started walking home, voice-messaging me for company. When she reached her driveway, she looked behind and saw the orbs were bigger and moving faster towards her. They were manifesting into full-spirit human beings. First, the head, then the shoulders, as the orb grew longer. Helena cried out and ran into the house. Later, having a cup of tea, she got the telltale pull on her head and lay down. Closing her eyes, it's extraordinary what she described - on the left of her screen, the Light Army was in a never-ending row marching towards her, and to the right of her screen, spirits waited to be released. As the army marched clouded in a green light, spirits exited in red as Helena released them to the Light.

She heard the song: Only You by *The Platters*.

Lyrics: *Only You can make all this world seem bright.*

Only You can make the darkness bright.

January 22nd: Wednesday, at 6:00 am, Helena woke to countless images of Jesus on the crucifix. She prayed, then as if the images were a backdrop for an intermission, she once again saw Catherine the Great and the armies walking towards her. She was made to watch it all, but nobody spoke to her. Throughout the day, as she closed her eyes, the flow of armies started again - at times rocking her body. They stopped if she got up to do something, but it flowed again as soon as she closed her eyes. She was urged to sit and close her eyes. Helena said she could hear the horses galloping if she stuck her fingers in her ears. "Irene, no wonder I have a headache; I have armies galloping in my mind." The next day, Helena closed her eyes and saw Catherine the Great turn to the side while ushering the armies through. Catherine was overseeing them. Before each army came through, their leader (the general or king) stood in front of them and presented himself to Helena. Some held their hats at their abdomen.

If Helena asked a question, Catherine turned and walked towards her, but the answer was a nod. The Flow was very important, and nothing was to get in its way. There was also a second row of men and women. They walked into the center of her screen and appeared to go through her. So, on the left were armies on horseback, and in the center were women and men. Helena got the impression that they might be scholars. She wasn't sure who they were.

Angels For Irene

January 24th: Every time Helena closed her eyes, she saw the Army of Light walking and dissipating in front of her. Helena bored easily and wanted to know what was going on. So, she came to my house hoping to record a channel with Catherine the Great. Helena had a family to care for, and Spirit wanted her eyes closed constantly. But if Helena thought she was busy before, this day would find her under more pressure. We made tea at 9:30 am, and Helena, blindfolded, sat beside me. We recorded a long channel (omitted). Then Helena said, "I see a beautiful rainbow tunnel," and out of it landed Archangels who fell to the ground and tucked their long wings behind them. Helena was astonished at the emerald green colour of Raphael. Other celestials were with them, and they spoke for a long time about me, that I was not to be afraid and one day I would see them. Helena continued to tell me what they were saying and said they were walking towards me. As she was telling me this, I received a text message from an acquaintance of mine - Michelle. We hadn't spoken for a while, and she knew nothing about Helena's experiences. Her message came out of the blue. Michelle said an angel came to her in a vivid dream. In her dream, I was crying, and the angel was behind me, holding me. She felt the angel wanted to let me know I was spiritually protected and loved. Michelle added that she felt its presence in her bedroom when she awoke. While I read Michelle's messages, the Archangels allowed me to feel their energy; they stood behind me, flapping their powerful wings. Feeling this breeze indoors while I sat on my living room couch was incredible. I can be heard on the audio saying excitedly, *"I feel you. I feel you."* It was a profound experience and one I hold dearly to.

They told me they were real in three ways – through Helena, Michelle (a third party), and sensation. Whenever I doubted what Helena was experiencing, I would remember this day and anchor my belief in these events. I know that this experience was orchestrated to do just that, propelling me to support Helena and write this book. You see, I fear ridicule, and I would never have written this book unless I experienced something myself – and after feeling them, I cannot or will not deny them. And I suspect they *knew* that!

The Almighty's Councillors

When the angels disappeared, Helena left to feed Belle before collecting Christopher at 1:40 pm. Arriving at the field, she was greeted by light beings saying they wanted her to close her eyes. She said she would, but only after picking Christopher up from school. When she returned to the field, she entered the stable and kicked off her shoes so the hay didn't stick to them. Then, the sky filled with angels and the field with light beings: Henry VIII, Catherine the Great, Knights of the Light, and lots of others. Then, a mist came down around her, and they said, *"Jesus is here."* They asked, *"When can you close your eyes and accept The Flow? It needs to be done. The Almighty wants it done. He is not happy."*

Helena didn't know what was going on, or why they were rushing her. There was a sense of urgency. *"I can do it at three o'clock. She repeated, "I can do it at three o'clock when I pick up James from school."* Then they said, *"He is coming,"* and Helena was confused. She knew Jesus was there because of the mist. Then they said, *"BOW."* Helena bowed her head, and then an unmerciful blast of air blew at her hard and fast. It blew right into the stable, lifting the straw up into the air. It was so strong it was shocking and nearly blew Helena over. It was a clear, bright day without a breeze, and this was an angry burst of air, *"Who can do that, Irene? She asked me later. Who can do that? I don't understand what is going on. What is the big hurry? They are telling me it is the Mighty One, and I need to accept a flow, but I have to collect James from school. Like what am I to do?"* After collecting her son James at 2:40 pm, she put the kids on Xbox and lay down to close her eyes. Rows of armies began rushing at her. A man came up to her with Catherine the Great and said, *"I am here to make sure this job is done! The order has come from He! This job has to be done, and it has to be done today!"* Helena lay down for the rest of the day; then, with eyes closed, she was met by new light beings, describing themselves as *higher* than the Hierarchy. She hit record on her phone, and they began to take her somewhere. Helena described what she was experiencing.

Helena: I see five or six light beings emanating the colour purple. They are seated on thrones.

Almighty's Councillors: *We are the higher. We are above the most.*

Helena: *What do you call yourselves?*

Almighty's Councillors: *We are the higher beings of the Light.*

The Almighty's Councillors, you see.

We are the highest of the most.

Helena: *They are all walking in front of me now; the one at the back is carrying a processional cross.*

Almighty's Councillors: *We are the highest of the high; you can go higher than we.*

Helena: *What is your message to me?*

Almighty's Councillors: *We are showing ourselves to ye.*

We are the Councillors for God, you see; we are his right-hand men.

What He says has to be done, Helena, your time has now come.

The Almighty, we are now taking you to He.

Helena was brought into a building. She was asked to follow the councillors to meet with the Almighty.

Helena: *Irene, huge ornate doors are opening - ornate designs like the chalices in a church. There are many people within the building.*

Helena: *Hello!*

Almighty's Councillors: *These are all people who work for The Mighty One.*

The Palace of The Light; do not fear you are here.

Helena: *They are all just coming out looking at me.*

Almighty's Councillors: *God has sent for you to come here. Stay close and follow me.*

Helena: *Do I follow you?*

Almighty's Councillors: *Yes, come through, we all have to greet you my dear.*

Councillors of the Light, yes, that's right!

You are at the top, the top of the above.

Congratulations, my dear, for getting through here.

God has been with you all through the way, all through your life.

We are all higher than the Hierarchy.

Helena: *There is a person here with a long train. He has been in the parades previously.*

Almighty's Councillors: *The Palace of the Light, the top of the top.*

For everything that has been said to you, it will all come true.

Well, my dear, do not fear; the time is near.

Helena: *I'm a little confused. What's going on?*

Almighty's Councillors: *Just follow us, come on.*

Helena: *I'm flying somewhere.*

Almighty's Councillors: *Come on, let's go, we have to go, now!*

Helena: Irene, *I'm still travelling through a pink cloudy tunnel, turning right and left and right and left.*

Helena: *Are we nearly there?*

Almighty's Councillor*: No, we are not there yet; this is quite long. Come on, Helena; you have to be strong. We are Councillors of the Lord. You must come at once.*

Helena: *My tummy is feeling a bit dodgy, Irene.*

Helena was nauseated as she was travelling very fast energetically. It seemed like she was travelling light years away through tunnels for a long time.

Almighty's Councillors: *This is the furthest you have ever been. It's light-years away.*

This is the furthest you will ever travel; this is the most.

We will be there soon. Come on!

Helena: *Tell them I feel a little bit sick.*

I heard Helena on the audio, trying to catch her breath. Her breathing was labored. She complained about being too cold one minute and too hot the next.

Helena: *Are we nearly there?*

Almighty's Councillors: *We will be there soon. Come on! Come on, just a little further on.*

Helena: *The gates of where? The gates of He?*

Almighty's Councillors: *Were nearly at the gates, to see The Almighty One you see; this is where He is.*

Helena: *Irene, I think I'm going to the Almighty One, I think?*

Almighty's Councillors: *To He you must travel; come on, you must go.*

You have to do what He says when He tells you so.

Beings of light, He makes us all shine bright.

Without Him, there would be no more, that is for sure.

Helena: *Who are you that is bringing me to Him?*

Almighty's Councillor: *I'm one of His Councillor men.*

Do not fear Helena; He will be nice to you.

Helena: *Are we nearly there yet?*

Almighty's Councillors: *Come on, we have got to go! We have got to go now!*

Take my hand, and I will help you come through. We have a big drop-down now, you see.

Helena felt sick, so took some deep breaths.

Helena*: Irene, down, down and down you go, and there is a big rush and back up again like you're on a roller coaster."* Helena continued to struggle.

Helena: *Are we here yet?*

Almighty's Councillors: *Walk behind me. Walk! Come on!*

Helena: *Wow! This is some journey.*

Almighty's Councillors: *Come on, walk up these steps. Right up to the gates, you see; they are right up in front of ye.*

Helena: *Oh! The whole council is here. The whole council is here. We are all walking up the steps.* (They showed her a chair.) *Oh! That's my chair? OK, I'll sit on my chair.*

Almighty's Councillors: **You are sitting with the Councillor men at the Table of Grace!**

Helena repeated this pointedly and with clarity. (They wanted her to repeat it; it must be documented.) Helena's last sentence was, *"I am at the right-hand side of The Great."*

Helena was told that she was being brought to God. But it sounded like she was brought to sit with the Councilors at His Table. However, a few moments later, I heard her gasp. I'm not sure what that gasp was in response to, as it was followed by silence on the audio. Later, Helena drew a picture of the building which sat on a cliff top. She believes it was The Palace of Light - the home of God.

Gods' Target

January 25th: The flow of armies continued to march and were joined by ordinary people. Catherine the Great said, "We have reached our target." So, whatever the Mighty One wanted the previous day, He got. That morning in the field, Helena looked up to see a circular opening in the sky; it flashed quickly, like if you flicked a paintball at a wall - a spikey flash. A bright circle of green light floated down from the sky, and out came four angels; two moved to the right and two to the left. Nuns wearing large rosary beads walked towards her. Behind them, light doors were opening. She then saw an image of the Sacred Heart while the nuns turned and walked back through the doors - *this was an introduction.*

After midnight, Helena voice messaged, "Irene, so sorry, I know it's late, but I have to tell you this. I was lying in bed watching The Flow when a huge throne appeared, and at its base was a tiny girl kneeling and bowing. The man on the throne just sat there for a minute, and I was smiling as He was so big and the girl was so tiny. Then He zoomed back from my screen and disappeared." Helena then asked Catherine, "Who was that? Catherine replied, "The

Mighty One. He was very pleased that we were on target." Helena was tickled pink. We are pretty sure that the little girl bowing at God's knee was Helena / Yvonne.

Helena was also shown The Flow; it was so fast it was like a tornado, and they stopped it to let her see what *she* looked like from *their* perspective. She said her third eye looked like a portal - a green circular opening, which they 'stepped up' into. Millions looked like they were passing through this tunnel. They showed her a bird's eye view of people walking in their thousands and travelling towards the portal. It was like a mass exodus from another world. And we did not know what this exodus was and where they were leaving. But I now believe they were earth-bound spirits leaving the earthly dimension. And I know this all seems crazy, but I have to write about what she saw because if I do not understand its meaning, it doesn't mean somebody else won't, and therefore I feel it needs to be written.

The Divine Heavens Fall

Guardians of Heavenly Gates

January 31st: Helena was in the field when light beings fell from the sky and walked toward her - angels were among them emanating green light. It started with two groups of four or five beings. In the second group, Helena was told to bow. She couldn't make out who they were, but they were important, and their lime-green and pink energy dissolved and rushed through her. This was the first time a spirit energy flow happened *outdoors,* as she normally saw it within the realm. She voice-mailed as it was happening. Catherine told Helena that the people who moved through her were – *"The Guardians of Irene and Helena's heavenly gates."* Nuns walked toward her two by two, then a bishop holding a crozier took a couple of steps forward, then moved to the right, where he sat on a chair. Doors opened behind him, and he disappeared through them. Helena had a vision of a child being lifted up by a spirit and then the child turning into a spirit. We didn't know at the time what it meant. But it was an introduction to what was to come. The energy 'atmosphere' grew dense in Helena's house, and the orbs kept coming but were breaking down instead of a sphere; they joined together in a 'river of energy' and flowed into anything containing water - even the dog's bowl. That night, she prayed for over two hours - water was a very important element as Helena prayed.

It's all Love

February 10th: Angels fell with a message for Helena saying God would fall to her, and she wasn't to be afraid because He could be very powerful and commanding. *"He is going to tell you what you're going to do, and the power of Him is going to go within you."* Later, she closed her eyes and saw a big door that looked like a tabernacle. Within that door was a throne, and someone sat on it. A couple of people were around the throne, one she believed was

Catherine the Great. Helena was told they were discussing *'She.'* Helena received a message:

 "It's all love; if you don't have love in your heart, there is nothing at all."

Then she heard a clear, physical voice saying, *"GOD."*

This was only a quick vision, sentence, and voice. At the time, I didn't even think it was important. But while writing this book, I realized that this was another *introduction!* Even God formally introduced himself. He was letting her know what He was about - LOVE and that He was next to appear.

February 11th: It was a cold winter day in Ireland, and we had snow. Helena sat on an upturned bucket inside the stable door to keep out of the wind. I heard Belle's hooves scraping the ground on the audio while Hank barked at the birds. She gazed at the sun, which looked like it was waving, and a black shadow moved across it. She hit record on her phone. Very bright colours formed in the sky, and Helena gasped. The shadowy clouds turned to deep purples, and she described a very bright blue, the brightest blue she had ever seen. These colours she had never seen before and were out-of-this-world. An orange light was among them, and she knew it to be Jesus. Light beings dropped down from the centre of these lights, and there were more beings than she had ever seen before. There were forty to fifty, maybe more, and as each one fell, they moved either to the right or left, leaving a space in the middle for the next one to fall, like actors on their curtain call waiting for the star to take centre-stage. In the centre, there were steps of light. For the next twenty minutes, the light display continued. Very little was said, but Helena wept on the audio at the beauty of their collective lights emanating together. She was overwhelmed with emotion as the heavens displayed their glory. As I said before, Helena was always shown the beings in visions or the realm before she met them, giving her time to adjust or to show an order, even an order of appearance. All the people whom she'd met as individuals or paraded themselves had come down together now. Among the celestials were: Archangels, Jesus, Our Lady,

Knights of the Light, the Almighty's Councilors, the Hierarchy, Yvonne Beauvais nuns, and God – who introduced himself the previous day. God was the last one introduced and the last one to show - centre stage, in glory.

An angel emanating a purple light walked up to her.

Angels of the Almighty: *Angels of The Almighty, we are falling to you, here He comes to you, with some of your nuns too.*

Jesus and Our Lady are present, too.

The divine heavens are falling to you.

All the Archangels, too.

As she waited, the wind blew, and I heard her say in astonishment, "The Almighty." She immediately recited the Lord's Prayer and, following it, wept. Whimpering, she said, "Oh, Wow! I have never seen so much brightness in my life. The colours are like the sun just opened up - gold and yellows sparkling so brightly. Sparkles are shooting everywhere. The brightest colours I have ever seen. Is that the way He is showing himself to me?"

She heard them say, ***"We came here to speak to you, to know that this is He."***

With that, the light blazed again in a display of sparkling iridescent gold and yellow light.

God spoke,

I am God, creator of earth.

I am The Almighty.

You will do my work for me.

I have granted you eternity.

You will follow through with all I will say to you.

Today is the day that will change your life.

You will never look at anyone the same again.

Helena: *It's like looking at a whole community. I see nuns opening and then closing doors. There are lots of nuns wearing long rosary beads. But I'm lost; I don't know what is going on. What's happening?*

Angel: *He's with you. Do you not feel him?*

He's with you. He's with you.

Helena: *This is too much.....this is too much.*

Helena was overcome, overwhelmed, and literally stunned by what she witnessed. The same pattern was played out - an audio message in the form of telepathy, a visual introduction, and then a visitation. This message was succinct and the basis for many messages she would receive. She was to remember and hold onto this message - *You will work for me and be granted eternity.*

The Chapel of Eternity

February 12th: Helena came to my house, and I made a pot of tea while she put on her eye mask. Helena described what she saw.

Helena: *I see an energy flow of colours; they are blending in a mixture of blue, green, and orange, and they are constantly changing. People are walking towards me and then step to the side. The colours change to bright blues and green. I see nuns floating on a beautiful river of blue light.*

Archangel Raphael: *Archangel Raphael, it's me and all the angels, too.*

The Angels of God, the angels of The Mighty One, we are all standing here.

All the nuns of you are here, too. Here is Our Lady, she is coming to you; and yes, she is in a dress.

Our Lady: *Hello, Helena, how are you?*

Helena: *The colours are changing again to red, blue, purple, and white. Now they are changing to orange. This is the orange light of Jesus.*

Archangel Raphael: *Jesus is now in the presence of you.*

Helena: *There are blue and white lights that are shimmering and misty, mixing like a disco light. They shine and flicker brightly. Angels are flying down and landing, and as they walk, the clouds change from blue to purple and white. The mist is turning slightly darker; it's red and cloudy but still shimmering.*

Angels of God: *The Angels of God, we are here to say, God is on his way.*

Angels of our Lord, there are a few.

Almighty's Councillors: *The Councillors of The Almighty One, we are here now.*

Representatives of He; this is we.

Community of the Heavenly.

Helena: *The Angels have huge wings.*

AOTHR: *Angels of the Heavenly Realms, we are here too;*

everyone is falling to you.

Someone said: ***When the Lord speaks, we all need to be here, my dear.***

Helena: *The colors are changing constantly and blending into one another. There are beams and beams of beautiful light. Blue, green, purple, and pink. Lots of beautiful lights emanating and mixing together.*

Angels of God: *He is on His way. Can you see the light?*

Knights of the Light: *Knights of the Light, we are here.*

He is on His way; do not go, stay.

Helena heard someone say: *The Gates of Heaven are opening now.*

Although hard to make out, Helena saw the outside of a building within the light. It looked like a castle, and its doors opened. People walked through the doors, and their individual pink, purple, and blue lights pulsed within the light encasing the castle. Helena knew when God was there because she said, "The brightness would blow you away."

Helena: *I am flying into the castle and joining the others. Queen Elizabeth I, Henry the VIII, and all the guides are here now. They are walking up either side of me, and I am going up the middle. We are walking into this building together. We are walking up the steps and entering under a large archway. Armored security guards are flanking the door. I am flying through a building.*

Angels: *We are flying with you.*

A Voice: *Nuns, bishops, popes, too,*

We're all here in front of you.

Helena: *A door is opening. It's God's building.*

Angels: *We are letting you see the Palace of Light you see.*

Helena: *There are big doors. They are huge, very detailed, and ornate. There are many nuns in front of me. The Knights of the Light are also wearing Armor.*

Knight of the Light: *We are showing you the Palace of Light,*

Knights of the Light, we shine so bright.

Helena: *You do indeed.*

Elizabeth I: *Elizabeth I, Henry VIII, Catherine the Great, we are all in the presence of Grace.*

Helena: *There are more doors and stained-glass windows as you see in a church. Lots of beautiful lights within. A staircase. We are going down corridors and hallways. There are more nuns in the halls. I'm now in a chapel with people wearing long draping garments (vestments) with a crucifix on the front of them. I'm told it's the* **Chapel of Eternity.** *This is where God grants eternity.*

Helena went on to give a brief description of The Palace of Light.

Helena: *The Palace of Light is enormous! Imagine the biggest palace you can think of and add on ten more. It has turrets and doors and stairs everywhere. I'm in an arched hallway; all the corridors and doors are arched, and nothing is square. The Palace is perched on a mountain with rocky landscapes; it's an actual other world. Every normal, decent, and good soul in the world goes to this world and the Gardens of God.*

After Helena left the Palace of Light, Catherine the Great said, *"You were at the gates of heaven today!"*

February 13th: Helena was told once again that God would be visiting her. She knew that the Community of the Heavenly gathered when He came, which took a while. Being practical, she took Belle out first and set her alarm for one hour. (Heaven had an hour). As her car was parked in the field and storm Ciara blew through Ireland, Helena sat sideways on her car seat, shielding herself from the wind. On the audio, I heard birds singing in the background and Belles's hooves scraping the ground.

Helena: *The sun is shining bright. I'm closing my eyes. I see the clouds moving apart. I see a bright blue color, but now it's changing to red. There is an opening of purple, and someone is dropping down already - it's Archangel Raphael. There's a yellow light, now it's green, changing to yellow, now yellow mixing with white. The yellow is coming towards me and moving to the side. It's all brightness and sparkles. Beams of yellow light are walking up.*

Archangel Raphael*: A few of us have gathered here already, you know.*

Waiting for your return, while you were out on your mare;

riding with care. We embrace you. Can't you see?

Helena: *I see lots of yellow, purple, and green lights, lots of brightness and iridescent sparkles. Beings are dropping down in beams of yellow light. They have gathered here already because they know how long the process normally takes. Everywhere is yellow and sparkling. The sun is shining on my face.*

Almighty Councillor*: Can you not see him? He is here. He's embracing you. We are the Councillors of He. He is on His way to you now. Be prepared and ready, you see. You have to listen to what He says to you. Everything He says will come true.*

Helena: *Now it's darker…cloudy…darker and colder. I see a being walking up to me, and it's getting colder.*

Archangel Raphael: *See His light? He shines so bright.*

Helena: *Now the light of a sun is shining on me, and it's sparkling.*

Archangel Raphael: *Your time has come. The Lord our God is standing in front of you.*

You will listen to all He says to you. It's getting colder, can you see?

The clouds are dropping for He. Anything you hear, you will have to say.

Your time is near; you will have to do jobs for He; this is true.

71

He will honor these jobs to you.

The power from within Him will be within you.

And the power from within Him will shine through from you.

Helena: *More people are coming and stepping aside, and they are saying, "I am in the presence of He." And I'm not surprised because everything is yellow, gold and cloudy. Light beings are moving within the cloud; these beings are gold and sparkling.*

Archangel Raphael: *Grace is right on your face.*

Helena: *It's a sea of yellow and gold iridescent light.*

Archangel Raphael: *He is standing at the Gates. He falls from the clouds to you;*

He takes the clouds with Him, too.

Helena: *That's why I feel the cold; it's the clouds dropping even though the sun is shining.*

Archangel Raphael: *The birds are singing with lots of cheer; they even know that God is here.*

God: *Your time has come, Helena Carroll,*

you will have to do the list of things that I will give to you.

On earth, you will do my work for me, and that is the way it's going to be, and that is the way it's going to stay! Until your dying day!

I'll say it once more to you. My light is going to shine through you.

I will greet you at the gates when you are done.

What I say is true, and these are the plans I have made for you.

The duties I will give you, you will follow through.

I am God, and I am speaking to you with everything that is, that you are going to do.

All the heavens surround you night and day, and this is the way it is always going to stay for you. On this earth, you'll remain until you return to me again. (Sounded like Agayn)

The world needs to change forever now, you know,

 because if it doesn't, there will be no place to go.

The darkness will not win me, my dear.

We are the brightest lights that anyone has ever known.

Helena*: Oh, it's getting colder. (*She shivered.)

God: *Do you see my bright light now? It is shining on you.*

You two girls have a lot of work to do.

Helena: *Oh, the light is so beautiful. (Helena was in awe.)*

God: *I am around you and Irene, too. I watch over all that you do.*

Tell Irene, Hi, from me. Good on her for the work she has done with you so far.

She has done a great job helping you, you know,

listening to you and telling you which way things will go.

She has got a beautiful energy, you know.

I need to go now, Helena, and return to the heavens, you see.

I embrace my light on you. I am the Heavenly Father, and this is how I shine through.

 Helena: *It's really cold; the brightness is going away and changing to misty purple and gold. The sun is shining, and it's all yellow and sparkling. They have stepped through the door.*

Helena was freezing as she sat at the edge of her car, her teeth chattering. When she got home, she put the kettle on for tea and sent a voice message. She couldn't believe what she heard and was crying. It was hard because I was at work and had to wait until lunch to speak to her. This was all so overwhelming. This message from God was slightly longer than the one before, but it stayed on message, elaborating as if easing her into what was going to unfold for her.

Master of Them All

February 17th: The orbs were still floating around Helena's house. She was praying as often as she could. It was annoying her as there were so many, and she was tired. It had taken over her life. I came to her house, and she put on her blindfold and talked to God.

Angels: *God wants to speak to you. Speak to you now, He will do.*

GOD: *Helena, my dear, do not fear; I am The Almighty, and I am here.*

Can you see? We are exploding with energy here.

I'm sitting on my throne. Can you see me now?

Everything you hear, my dear, everything you see, everything I say,

you must speak the words out your mouth; there is no more hanging about.

I am God; can you see me on my throne?

My dear, this is me. I am your God, you see. I appear to you now.

With all the heavenly fathers, they are around.

All the priests and the bishops, the councillors of Me;

We are all here, you see.

I am the Almighty, the creator of all.

74

I will never fall from where I sit, for where I sit, this is where I stay.

I look over this earth every day. I am here for you in every way.

Can you see us all here, the bishops and all?

We are all very tall; I am God, the Master of them all.

For I am the King of Heaven. I control the heavens up here, you see.

My dear Yvonne, that's who you were, you see.

Her soul is in Helena Carroll's body.

Helena, you will be able to connect with Yvonne.

For the love is inside of you too; Yvonne is a very big part of you.

She was a saint on this earth before, and she is coming back to do my work from within you. This is why I have fallen to you.

You are the chosen person on earth, you see, for Yvonne to go within ye.

I am The Almighty. I have spoken to you, now I must go.

I will leave you with the Councillors of The Heavenly Fathers."

Helena: *The councillors are singing.*

Councillors of God: *We sing up here all the time, you know.*

This is the way our spirits sing to you in prayer. That's what we do.

Councillors of Heaven, we are coming through to you.

The Lord is my Shepard; there is nothing I shall want.

These words are very important in prayer; say them with care.

Heavenly Father, we sing to thee: creator of earth is He.

This is an incredible journey you are on; you must stay strong.

Our Lady spoke: *Tell Irene you have spoken to the Heavenly Councillors.*

They are singers in heaven.

End of channel.

Helena imitated their tone and sang with the councillors. In this message, God reiterated what Luther said before, that Helena had Yvonne's Beauvais soul in her body. God made sure Helena knew what was going on. God stayed on message.

Spirits Queue

Feb 27th: Helena was outside her cottage complaining to Stephen about the amount of praying she had to do. She was fed up and tired of praying constantly, and the number of orbs never lessened; they were growing in number. Looking over Stephen's shoulder, she saw a person's spirit walking toward her. Its subtle energy body was green like the orbs, but it had the full form of a human being. Behind that spirit was another that moved in behind the first, then another that moved in behind the second - forming a queue. It seemed to only hit Helena when she saw spirits in their human form that they were lost and searching for the Light. She felt so guilty she cried, and realizing she had a job to do, went in to pray.

 Later, she told Stephen, "I forgot to feed the horse, but I don't want to go to the field in the dark as there might be spirits manifesting." Helena was right; when she did go down, people started walking into the field. They didn't scare her, though, as they formed an orderly queue. She told them to go in fours. She prayed, and four dissolved into the horse's water through. When she finished her prayers, she said, "The rest of you follow me home." Helena seemed to take forever to grasp concepts, changes, or new ideas. Even though she had been releasing spirits as orbs, it was only hitting her then that they were real people who were stuck.

The Almighty's Congregation

February 28th: In the afternoon, Helena sat at the edge of the stable on an upturned bucket, recording what she saw.

Helena: *There is a blanket of misty cloud backlit by a yellow light, and angels are falling from it. I see a portal in a cloud and a cloud behind that, like a wall and a hole in that wall. The colours are purple, pink, and orange. I see the large wings of an angel and a lady in a big dress. There are people walking through. They are coming in as energetic colors, then changing into form, and are walking toward me again like yesterday. It's like an energy flow. There are more falling with sparks of light as the energy comes through. There are big swirling colors of light - yellow lights are still falling through clouds, with pink and lime green sparks. It's getting colder. An angel is walking right up to me. Lime green beings are landing in front of me; their colours are turning pink and red, and more are coming through. Someone is walking in front of me.*

Knight of the Light: *It is me, the Knight of The Light, that's right! Can you not make out?*

Can you not see?

Helena: *It's quite hard. You are in the clouds. I see nuns. They understand. They look back at me. Oh! They can hear. They look back again. (Helena chuckled).*

Nuns: *This is no laughing matter, my dear; this is your reality here,*

who you are and what you're going to be;

a medium is a little thing for you, you see.

Helena: *A white light is coming.*

Catherine the Great: *Catherine the Great, it's me. Can you not see?*

Helena: *I see a circle of beautiful colours and a door opening. The Knight of Light stands to the side, and bright lights come out and stop in front of me. It's hard to make out their form. I think they are maidens; their colours are orange and gold. A man wearing lots of robes with chains across his chest is showing himself in all his glory. They are turning around so I can see them. It's hard to make out their outlines. People are coming out from behind a curtain as if on stage.*

Helena questioned who they were because nobody was telling her.

Then a voice said: *The Almighty's Congregation.*

Helena: *They're saying heaven is here. 'It's like a big cloud; people are walking out from the cloud and showing themselves to me. Some are ladies wearing big dresses. There could be different types of nuns, too. They bowed to me. There is a bright yellow swirling light. Somebody is walking up through the middle. They could possibly be men.*

Congregation: *We have all fallen from heaven here to you today.*

Helena: *They have turned sideways, and there are so many. There are nuns, priests, maidens, kings, queens and, soldiers in armor, a beautiful angel.*

Angels of Heaven: *Angels of heaven, we are here too.*

We are Angels of heaven, Helena, can't you see?

Helena: *I can see you. You are very beautiful. Hello! Hello!*

Helena: *There are four small angels flying in front of me. People are standing back to let someone else through. Irene, people keep coming, and their lights are so beautiful and bright; it is very hard to make out who they are.*

Helena was in awe and felt close to tears with the beauty of what she saw. She wondered why they were not talking to her. Normally, at home, in meditation, or when channeling, the spirits first walk out showing themselves, then turn and walk away. Later, after they have first appeared, they come back and introduce themselves. Here, the same format was played out. But the people from heaven fell to her OUTSIDE; she saw them fall through the clouds.

Someone spoke: *We will talk to you, my dear, we are very near.*

We will introduce ourselves to you.

Heavenly Congregation: *We are heavenly maidens of the sky, nuns, soldiers, heavenly angels. This is true; we are flying in front of you.*

Helena: *These are people who live in heaven; some are scholars. A door opened in front of me, and everyone came out. They are walking toward me, and their colours are spectacular. Their forms break down into energy - an ice-blue colour. Beings are walking up now in red and orange light right in front of my face, but I cannot make them out. In silence, they walk into me. The door closes, and it slides to a side. Like four doors on a stage, the door slides to the right as people leave a door. Then another one opens. Curtains are pulled to the side.*

Again, it is only now, as I write this book in June 2021, that I realize that this was also a *formal introduction* and that the Heavenly Congregation were coming to earth. You will see as the book unfolds, that these were to be heavenly workers. They were councillors, priests, maidens, nuns, angels, soldiers, Knights of the Light, and probably other people too.

A Saint You Will Be

February 28th *continued:* Helena was given a message.

A saint you will be, my dear.

The Heavenly Congregation is here, you see.

We're supplying you with heavenly energy.

You will let the world know, that God is back you know.

You will reunite Him to the earthly.

Messages from He, that God is the savior of all of Ye.

This we will all do, and this is why we are all coming through you.

Heavenly Father, beneath the earth, beneath the soil, they pump for oil.

(Helena thought she heard Iraq… The wind was noisy.)

The cruelty on this earth is beyond a joke.

The human race has a lot to answer for.

Humanity needs to know what they have done, and the time has come, for the Creator to land on earth, you see, within society.

You, my dear, will be the representative of He.

It's true this will be a challenge for you.

We all have faith in you.

We're giving you everything you need to succeed.

For you to grow, we tell you so.

Life on earth will never be the same again.

Unless He comes back down to earth, you know.

We will snap everybody out of this, you know.

You represent He, my dear; you will be Godly.

The beauty of He will be within you, and it will all shine through.

The path you're going on, my dear, is bigger than the hemisphere. (Helena giggled.)

Life as you know it will never be the same for you; this is so very true.

We said it before, and we will say it again:

Life for you will never be the same again.

We are finished with you now, my dear, you may go;

we will see you again tomorrow, you know.

Maidens of the sky that where we,

we just filled you in, in what you're going to be.

Heavenly Fathers, councillors, you see.

Knight of The Light, don't forget me.

The Congregation of He.

We have all been here; now we will disappear.

End of message.

Helena: *There is an opening in the sky, and they are breaking down and going in. There's something in the sky with great big wings! It has a huge wingspan! It's a giant angel! It opened, and they were all going in through a sparkling circular opening that was shrinking. It's getting smaller and smaller and disappearing. The cloud has closed, and it looks like a normal cloud. Wow! I can see people walking into the cloud. It's all shimmering. That was awesome!*

She heard Michael Jackson's song – You Are Not Alone.

Divine Angel

Over the following days, Helena continued caring for her children and Belle. Looking skywards, she witnessed the enormous angel, which they called – a Divine Angel. In its chest was a circular opening, and from him flew angels and from them more angels. There were rivers of energy flowing down toward her, and she was freezing. It's impossible to explain all these flows; the best we can understand is that spirits are energetic light forms that can break down into a collective energy that can flow. This energy flowed toward Helena for weeks. There were maidens and angels entering a castle doorway within the clouds, and through the doors, she saw hallways. Knights of the Light guarded the flows. There were little angels with yellow lights flying around them and around Helena's feet in an ice-blue light. Helena saw a clearer image of the Knights of the Light. They wore gloves that went halfway up their arms, capes that gathered at their shoulders, armor, and helmets. Songs were played for Helena as she sat receiving flows; she heard Gold by Spandau Ballet; its lyrics *Always Believe in your soul.*

Our Contract

March 3rd: Helena had her hair done, and after collecting her boys from school, she heard an angel say, "Your hair is lovely." She laughed. Then she heard the song The Greatest Love of All, by Whitney Houston. She went to the field, and it was a bright day. She saw figures in the clouds and the field. Jesus and Our Lady appeared.

Helena: *Who am I in the presence of today?*

Angels of our Lord: *The heavens will fall today; they are on their way.*

The earth is in trouble Helena in a big, big way,

God is not happy with the way it's run today.

Greed and poverty are all over, you see,

and a change needs to be made before the world ends, you see.

God will come down through you,

and you will let the world see that God did fall to ye.

There's no time to waste, you see; this is the word from The Almighty.

Letters of love He sends to you; He knows his girls will pull through.

Abide for the contract you did sign for He; that is the law up here, you see.

Once you put your name on paper, you must do everything that He asks of you.

Contracts are non-void, you see, not when you work for He;

with the Devil, that may be.

Lies and evil that is true, the work of the devil you don't want to have to do.

Satan is here, that is for sure. You see him in all the bad things you see, evil, gluttony, greed; they sin and sin and sin some more.

Satan doesn't care about you; Satan doesn't care what the people do.

He's happy for them to be the worst that they can be because that satisfies He.

God is different in many ways; the light of God will stay.

Bask in His glory, you two. Never get pulled by the Devil, you see.

Money can change people; don't let this change you; stay honest in everything you do.

Honesty is the best policy you see; that is a message from God to ye.

My dear girls, it won't be long now before you show the world how.

How important God is to all of ye.

The people in the darkness must open their eyes and see

that He is here, He is great, and He will come to save the human race. Destruction that they do to themselves, you see, is a constant reality. The world is in big trouble if it keeps going the way it is.

Helena, my dear, you will see, too, the essence of God flowing through you.

You will feel the power from within His heart, and that power with you will never part. You will go on until your dying day, and in the name of God, you will stay.

Known to people on this earth, you see, that God did fall and come through ye.

The Almighty, how amazing He is, this is true.

He created the world for me and you.

He stood by and let everyone grow, and they have turned onto a different path, you know. A path of destruction, they ripped the world apart, you see. Trying to make money from anything you see.

Cruelty to animals: this is true; there's cruelty to animals all around you.

Children, it disgusts Him what they do, what they do to poor children, you see. These animals won't live to Eternity.

Fall, fall, fall they will go; and the light of day again, they will never know.

In the darkness, they will loom forever more, that is for sure.

There's no way out of there, you see. If you sin, this is where you will be.

Floating in nothingness for evermore.

That's the Word of The Lord.

End of message.

The Divine Angel, surrounded by flying angels, hovered in the sky, and the light of Our Lady and Jesus walked into its centre which radiated a yellow light. People walked toward Helena and flowed into her while accompanied by Knights of the Light. (Helena drew a rough drawing of this angel. If you can picture a hummingbird hovering vertically and look at its breast - imagine there is a circular/oval opening in the breast; that is where the entrance to the Divine Angel was located.) Helena continued to sit on a bucket outside the stable. Angels hovered over the people who were walking in a queue toward Helena. These people were emanating the purest and brightest white light. Helena said, "They came in all their glory."

Gods Heart

March 13th: The previous night, in visions, Helena was shown a religious book and believed the book was significant. Again, we think it was the Bible - *a visual introduction of what was to come.* She went to the field, sat on an upturned bucket, and looked skywards. A cloud of sparkling energy floated down. Feeling a pull on her forehead, she knew they were going to connect. The birds were singing, and Belle was chewing hay in the stable behind her.

Helena: *Beings are falling within a lime green colour, and people are walking toward me. I can't make out who they are because it is so cloudy.*

A minute or two passed while the celestials gathered.

God: *Helena, my sweet, the Almighty is here; we would like to speak to you.*

The power invested in me; I invest in you.

God began to display a vibrant light.

Helena: Oh Wow! It's a beautiful light! It's a vibrant, pinky-red light!

God: *This is my heart of love I present to you now.*

I display to you my heart, my dear; do not fear, I'm always near.

Helena*: Irene, it's so beautiful! It's glowing, and I have never seen this colour before. Wow! Wow!*

Helena began to cry as the beauty of God's Light overcame her.

God: *The Love I have for you grows and grows each day;*

and this love will always stay.

And yet again, you shed a tear, my dear.

Helena laughed through her tears.

God: *You are the chosen one for me; you are the chosen one you see.*

Believe in everything that you hear, see, and say;

for I am the Almighty, and I am here to stay.

To stay with you and guide you, it's true.

Guide you over the next year or two.

Helena: *Irene, the display of lights is so beautiful. It's like a pinky-red strobe lighting display. Now I hear music, the song is* Because You Loved Me, *by* Celine Dion.

God: *You will spread the light for me;*

you will spread the light for mankind to see.

Almighty's Councillors: *The Lord is my Shepard; there is nothing I shall want. (Is sung by the Almighty's Councillors).*

The light display ended.

End of message.

God had visited Helena, displaying the light of His heart. I believe He wanted her to fully experience and remember Him because her work was about to begin, and she would need all her strength to carry it out. Holding onto these beautiful memories would bring her comfort in the future.

The Calm Before the Storm

Portal to the Higher Realms

March 14th: It was a cold, rainy and windy day. The coronavirus was sweeping the country. In the field, Helena fed Belle and only had a couple of minutes because the weather was so bad. A couple of minutes was all that was needed.

Helena: *I look down through my third eye, and I see a portal. I look up in front of me, and I see a portal and cloudiness."* Then she heard,

A portal is now opened to you, my dear.

More spirits will be able to communicate with you, my dear.

It is true what we have just said to you; the portal is clearly open to you.

You will begin feeling more spirits communicating with you.

These will be from the higher realms you see; deceased of the living they will be.

The more you release, the higher you will go, my dear.

The higher realms will start feeding more through you now, my dear.

Do not fear, my dear. This will be in a controlled situation for you.

Helena: *Who is it that I am speaking to?*

Catherine the Great: *Catherine the Great, my dear.*

Helena: *Hi Catherine.*

Catherine the Great: *This is all we wanted you to know; now we must go.*

Helena: *Will I feel fear?*

Catherine the Great: *You won't feel fear. You will be just more open to spirits feeding through.*

End of message.

In the afternoon, Helena lay down and closed her eyes and saw Catherine the Great in a realm standing beside three doors. Catherine said, *"You need to release more for these doors to be fully opened to you."* Later, when Helena closed her eyes, she saw a 'realm or a space', and within this space, an angel stood. People gathered in this space as if they were in a train station going somewhere. Helena prayed, and suddenly, there were sixteen doors in a semicircle, each opening and closing alternately as if someone was controlling the number of people coming through. At first, we didn't understand the significance of these doors, but they were doors to higher realms where spirits were gathered and stuck. This was the beginning of mass spirits being released.

The Coronavirus

March 15th: Helena was in the field when she received a message from God.

God: *The end of this world is very near. The human race needs to change its way; the way they approach the earth on their day-to-day.*

The coronavirus, yes, this is me; it's here now for the world to see.

How quickly the coronavirus can wipe out so many.

There are too many on this earth, you know. This world can combust, you know.

The coronavirus can keep a steady flow, a steady flow of population, you see; deceased, there will be many.

It's a controlled environmental thing, you see. It's the world's destiny, the coronavirus, you see. I control everything on this earth, as you know, and I can make this coronavirus go.

And this I will do, you will see. The coronavirus will disappear as quickly as it has come.

This will not touch you and Irene, you see; I protect you for me.

For you to fulfil what I want you to do.

In time, you will see, and in time, you will know when this coronavirus will go.

I can control this at will; you see, this whole virus is because of me.

I allowed this to happen, you know, this is the way it has to go.

Epidemic there has to be, population control there must be.

Every hundred years or so. I set off a virus down here below.

Cruel, it may seem, but it needs to be; I control this universe, you see. I will stop this, you know, you will see it is true; I will stop this between me and you.

The world will stand up and see that I am here, and this is me, The Almighty. On this earth, your name will get known, known for The Girl that God Fell to, you see.

Wait until you see everything that you are going to do, what you're going to say, what you're going to hear; within a very short time, this coronavirus will disappear.

End of message.

The Orbs Multiply

March 22nd: Helena saw more orbs forming in her house and heard individual voices as she drifted off to sleep. Then, a group of spirits began walking around her house. She didn't know who they were, but they seemed to work for the spirit world, and she didn't know why they had come. We had no idea what was going on. We believed the growing activity in her cottage had something to do with the portals being opened. This turned out to be true.

May is the Month for You

March 24th: Helena was at home when she felt a strong presence, so she closed her eyes to connect.

Elizabeth I: *You are speaking to Elizabeth the Great above.*

I'm your true guardian up here, you see.

But things will develop for you, you see. Have faith in us up here, my dear.

In may it will be all crystal clear; that's how many weeks you have left, you see.

Keep doing what you do every day on earth, my dear.

Keep releasing spirits to us; this is true; this is a must.

We clap our hands for the wonderful work you did, my dear; we cheer. In around the month of May, you will see, and you will know.

Communion cancellation for James Thomas, you know.

But don't worry or hesitate, my dear; in May, it will all become clear.

End of message.

(Helena's son, James Thomas, had his First Holy Communion cancelled.)

A Lot of British Society Will Die

March 25th: While in mediation, Helena received a message from Catherine the Great.

Catherine the Great: *Repeat all I say when I say it to you.*

Catherine the Great, yes Helena, it is me, looking down upon the world we do see.

Coronavirus will wipe out a good few; your country is so small, you see.

A lot of deaths on your little island there will be. Ireland will step and fight back, you see; this virus won't overcome you like it did in Italy.

Everyone will stay in now, you see; everyone is afraid of what could be.

The United Kingdom will have a rough going over, my dear.

It will spread rampant over there, you see;

a lot of British society will die, my dear.

There will still be restrictions on travelling, you see.

Travelling to other countries that won't be anywhere near my dear.

Global warming is destroying the earth, you see,

We have to raise our hands for the world to see, the world will combust and disappear.

End of channel.

In the realm, Helena was again shown lots of doors within a frame. People were entering and exiting these doors, some of whom she recognized as the Hierarchy. Helena was made to watch this activity but didn't know why. Her house was filling with energy, and the deceased continued to walk into her garden. She noticed one man wearing a suit and a woman in high heels. For the following few weeks, little seemed to be happening. It was difficult for us as we waited for further instructions from the celestials. Helena and I had a falling out over some misunderstanding, and our nerves were strained. I decided to start writing a children's story to pass the time during lockdown. One day, while washing the kitchen floor, Helena closed her eyes and, on her screen, saw a portal with a cloud of energy spinning rapidly through it. She believed her house was filling with spirit, which was then leaving through this spinning portal. We were soon to learn that Helena was right! It was unusually quiet during this time, and the realm was empty, as was the field; only angels hovered over it. She constantly heard - *pray and release*. Then, one day, she observed angels and shadows of people walking toward a light in the sky and a door closing within a cloud. She realized angels were escorting spirits in the realm and outside.

April 24th: The cottage was buzzing with energy. Helena said, "It's like lots of bees buzzing around." She released spirit all day, then asked someone to help her because there were so many waiting to be released. The energy was still spinning in the portal.

New Vision & Guides

Helena is Allowed to See More

April 29th: In the field, Helena sat and watched the deceased walk over to the horse trough and then rise out of the trough as energy. Angels carried this energy to a door in the sky. By evening, they allowed her to see more. This time, the deceased *walked* back from the horse trough and were greeted by angels who lovingly put their arms around them before flying upward. It was very beautiful.

Everyone Will Step Before Me

May 12th: Helena had a vivid dream - she was in our father's house, which was filled with spirits wanting to be released. She saw a priest with long dark hair; he was a black man dressed in tribal attire – a warrior of some sort. She woke with a droning buzz in her ear, like a high frequency that hurt her. This was once again a *visual introduction*. It was Herou - he was a new guide for Helena. Over the following days, he connected with Helena, and she saw people queuing to see him. He was stamping something, and I wondered if they were the cards Helena saw in one of her first dreams. He told her, "Your guides can change in a day."

May 21st: Helena connected with Herou, asking if he was guiding and controlling the spirits around her,

Herou: *Yes, this is true. I have spoken to you, I told you. This is where I stay.*

Spirit protector, you see, spirits around you. I protect you from them, too. I am the vice president of this company, you see. I know how difficult this can be for you.

It is not easy being bombarded as much as you do, so I protect you from all that comes to you.

I am here, and I am here to stay throughout your spiritual journey,

for as long as I need to be here for you.

This is my job, and it is nice to meet you, Helena.

Candidates, there will be a few, especially the ones that are needed to help you.

I will be one of these candidates, you see. There won't be just me. There will be two or three.

We will help you with the most difficult ones you see.

The darker ones that don't want to let go.

We will assist you to release them, you know.

This is all ahead of you. My name is Herou, and here I will stay with you.

This is our job here on earth, you see, protectors of you and what you will do.

Yes, the angels told you they take care of you. Darkness is all around you.

Where there is darkness, there is light; stay within the light like you do.

Brighter than bright, and the darkness will not appear. Keep your vibrations high, my dear.

For another few months, they will keep coming to you.

I am here to stop any problems you see; they must step before me.

All over the summer, my dear, you will just have to get used to it,

they will come in their droves to you.

But I am here to prevent any problems you see. Everyone will step before me.

I am a priest, man, you see. Only the Light has the right to come to you.

Darkness will prevail, but I am here to clear them away from you. No darkness will enter your home, you see. That must bring you some comfort now, my dear. To know that I am here. No need to feel fear, my dear. No one will hurt you here. They are just lost souls. They are drawn to you. You are a light that they can see, a light so bright, they can see for miles around you. The Angels of the Lord hover over you.

All the souls are drawn to you. This job you will still have to do.

Until a time comes to an end for you. But then on, you will have the ability to release a few; the ones that are meant for you.

Pedestal, that is where they have got me. I am a warrior and a very spiritual man.

Baptised priest I am. So, I am a holy man.

End of channel.

As the house was packed with spirit, Helena asked them to leave at night. Herou said, *"The ones who got there first will stay; they are in a queue."* When she prayed, they flew like a river of energy from everywhere, even through walls and mirrors. It was like a race to the bowl of water. In the realm, Catherine stood at a light door, and orbs passed through it as if on a conveyor belt; this soon changed, and the orbs changed shape into human form and walked through. The odd spirit tried to talk to Helena, and some asked, "Where are we?"

May 21st: In the evening, Helena was playing with Christopher when Herou connected.

Herou: *What will come ahead of you will be spectacular, you see; now you have the backing of me.*

Just know that you are protected, and we will put you on the right path you know.

Don't worry or fret like you did today.

You feel alone, but you are not on your own; we penetrate your mind, you see; this is the power of We.

Capabilities, my dear, you have a few; don't ever underestimate you; the wonderful gift that has been given to you.

And you are quite capable of fulfilling it, too. The spirit world supports you in all that you do.

Just know there is a lot of us here depending on you.

We all work accordingly; you see, we all work for He, the Almighty, my dear; He is here.

He is clear in what he expects from all of We. He is the creator of all of us too, and every one of us has a job to do. He's invested in me, just like he has invested in you.

Keep releasing spirits to us, my dear; that is your job now down there.

I just wanted to say thank you from us up here.

Light years ahead, we have been in connection with you.

You may go now, my dear; the pressure will ease too.

End of channel.

As Helena channelled Herou, she felt a strong pressure in her head. He had come through to comfort her as she'd been fretting. The frustrated and impatient spirits didn't want to wait any longer to go to the Light. Some asked for help while others bumped the bed, causing Helena to lose her temper. Shouting at them, she took the bowl of water from her bedroom into the kitchen. Then, returning to bed, she stuffed cotton wool in her ears to block out the spirits cries for help.

An Angel Pointed to the Sky

May 25th: Helena was seeing more of the events surrounding her. As she prayed, it was Herou she saw in her mind's eye. A queue of people walked up to him, and he placed his hand on each person's shoulder as they walked through a door behind him. Later, sitting in her back garden praying, she saw angels and a doorway in the sky.

 An angel came to her and said:

We love you in every way;

you can hear what we say.

He pointed to the sky, so she focused her attention there and saw deep within the clouds, many shimmering, sparkling angels and a very large light being and a doorway within him. She'd seen the door close.

Archangels Comfort Helena

May 26th: Helena voice mailed saying she was still concerned about the spirits trying to communicate with her at night. She remembered her night of terror and didn't want it to happen again. I couldn't blame her. As we spoke, she felt a presence – it was Archangel Michael. Closing her eyes, she saw four male warrior angels. Michael said, "Follow us," and she followed him through beautiful coloured tunnels.

Archangel Michael: *Archangel Michael, can you see?*

Don't feel afraid, my dear, you are not alone;

they just all want to come home.

They get frustrated because they are lost, you see,

appreciate your gift, my dear; to you, they do not appear.

You hear them; yes, this is true; we can't stop them from trying to get through.

Help with the situation we will try to do.

You work with the spirit world now; you see, spirits are all around you; you are releasing them to me. I meet them at the gates, you know, I show them where they have to go.

Frustrations there are for you, but this is what you have to do.

A couple of months remain now, you see; they do not harm your family.

You need to fulfill what you have to do until you reach the target that is meant for you. From then on, you see, it will get a lot more easy.

For the seen and the unseen, my dear, I think we have made it very clear. You need to let go of your anxiety, you see. That's not up to us up here. Suggestions: we can make a few; you need to muddle through. Be focused on releasing to us, you see.

When you hit your total, they will stop coming to you, and that's not far away from you. This is the door to the unknown, you see; come on in and follow me. Come through; we will show you. (Helena was shown another tunnel of bright white light.) The emperors and pledged saints, doorways one to your left, this is the doorway that lies ahead for you, all the seen and unseen concerning you; this we mustn't take you through.

Your path out is made for you; your future will be amazing, you see.

You have to finish your path on this journey.

Light years away through time now, you see, this is the light you just did see.

Through here is the way you go when you have passed over, you know.

Light years ahead, you know, these are the tunnels that lay ahead of you.

Anxiety and pain, you have to let go.

Fifteen thousand, my dear, that is how much you need to put through.

It is dwindling numbers for you. It won't be long before you hit your target, my dear.

Between now and then, you know what you will have to do.

End of channel.

Helena described channeling Archangel Michael and the heavenly beings as a "Stream of loving energy flowing through her." It felt beautiful, and their gentle essence would be reflected in her tone of voice.

The Heavenly Congregation

Baptisms

Later, while praying in her garden, Helena closed her eyes, focusing on the energy around her. Two angels stood at her children's paddling pool. Curious as to why they were there, she rose and walked to another part of the garden to get a different perspective. One angel turned and bowed to Helena, and she bowed back. The angels were bending over doing something, but she couldn't figure out what. More angels waited along the outskirts of the garden. Then she saw something extraordinary - an energy shooting into the pool, but when it rose, it was the head and shoulders of a person. Each angel placed a hand on the person's shoulders. Looking around, she noticed two queues of people - one entering the front entrance to her cottage and the other from the front entrance of our father's house. Each spirit knelt between the two angels, dipped their head into the water, and was handed over to waiting angels upon rising. Those angels accompanied the spirit skywards where the large light being that Helena saw the previous day waited. Each spirit walked through its doorway, followed by the next. This is why the angel had pointed to the sky the day before - to show Helena where they were going. It was a large angelic transporter. *Bit by bit, day by day, they were showing her more.* Knights of the Light were also in the field, and Helena found it hard to focus on them because their beautiful spirits flashed like strobe lighting.

The Lord Almighty

In the afternoon, while out horse-riding, Helena brought Belle to a different field to eat fresh grass. Helena and I were voice messaging each other, when something amazing happened. She told me afterwards that she was glad she had the phone in her hand so she could describe what she saw *as* it was happening. In her message, her voice was shaking, and she was crying.

Helena: *Irene, Irene, you're not going to believe this! I am here on my horse in a field down the Burrow Road. And I see something moving towards me; it's like a large circle of energy, and it's coming closer. I can see a big pair of hands held in the prayer position within flowing sleeves and the outline of a man's head. He is bowing to me, and I keep bowing back. We just keep doing this. I don't know what else to do, Irene. He is sparkling and twinkling. We just keep bowing to one another. I see another opening behind Him in the clouds and a door in the clouds. I see a staircase, and four light beings exit the door, walk down the steps, and stand to the right. Then they turned and walked back up the staircase and back through the doorway; this is crazy stuff, Irene. They have closed the door. Why are they showing me these steps? Just clouds and mist and walking; they wanted me to see it.*

Then she heard: *The Lord Almighty. The Lord Almighty. The Lord Almighty.*

Then she heard the being speak.

God: *My child of Grace with the beautiful face;*

To you here, I wanted to appear.

Helena: *He's back again, and He is bowing to me. There are bubbles of energetic auras filled with angels hovering in the one spot all around Him. They are hovering in the shape of an arc, like a rainbow.*

We tried to comprehend the heavenly events that Helena was witnessing. Her initial ability to communicate with a spirit, which at first amazed us, was now insignificant. Our heads were spinning with the rapid development of unfolding events, which continued to amaze us.

Release, Release, and do Not Fear

May 27th: In the morning, while Helena was home praying, she felt a pull on her forehead. It was Herou.

Herou: *You've seen it now, and now you know it's all true.*

You truly are hardworking, you know, the amount of souls to date that you have let go.

Keep concentrating on releasing to We.

We can't help but see how frightened you can be.

Last night, you tried so hard, my dear; we know for your fear, you have to let it go.

Keep concentrating on doing this, you see; it's a part of you now, my dear.

You have to set them all free until you reach that total you see.

Then, you will blend back into society.

Keep releasing, keep releasing, you must see,

and eventually, from these spirits, you will soon be free.

Hit your total, my dear; just keep focusing on what you see. That is all I wanted to say.

Release, release, and set them free; they are calling to you, and you can hear them, too.

Let them go now; that is all you must do. God Bless You.

Release, release, and do not fear.

End of channel.

Ladies of the Divine and Saints

May 27th: 8:30 pm, and Helena was sitting in her garden eating an ice pop. She viewed a nun accompanying a male spirit to the paddling pool where two angels waited. The man knelt and was baptized, and when he rose, the angels put their hands on his shoulders and brought him back to the nun. She then brought him to the waiting angels. These angels were hovering and flew the deceased into the sky, where their transport awaited. The angels who hovered in the sky behind her house differed from those who hovered out front.

It was a beautiful evening, and at 9:20 pm, Helena went to feed Belle. Immediately, shimmering oval auras floated down in front of her. Within them were ladies dressed similarly to Our Lady (they were very faint). They twirled around so she could see them better, and then they curtsied. They told her they were *Ladies of the Divine and Saints*. More oval auras appeared, and within them were Knights of the Light. They asked Helena to start releasing spirits. As Helena picked up Belles's droppings, she prayed. I was at home typing away, waiting for her to finish. Soon, she told the ladies she had to go as it was getting dark. They floated down, curtsied, and bowed. There were other males dressed in robes; they floated down while blessing themselves with the sign of the cross. They floated around her, bowing constantly, saying, *"We are Christian Saints, my dear. Now, we may leave you and go."* Helena bowed back and recited two Hail Mary's. They hovered over to her car, bowing constantly. Helena found it hard to pronounce 'Christian' and repeated it a couple of times in the voice message, so I heard it correctly. I was once again in shock.

While driving home, she voice messaged, recording everything she saw. Pulling into her garden, more beings waited for her. She saw these with her own eyes, not through her third eye. They were not the angels she was used to seeing in her garden; they were bigger. She said, "I am getting out of the car to get a better look." It was a bright evening, but the light was dying at 22:10 pm. The angels moved toward her and said, '*We are the Angels of the Lord.*' Then, they turned and stood in a row - one turned and bowed to the angel beside him and offered him something, and the other angel in line took what was offered, then he turned and bowed to the next angel. There were lots of nuns as she saw habits and what Helena called draping cloth. Helena couldn't make out what it was they were passing. A light door opened, and they walked through it. Surrounding the door was a curtain that seemed to open and close. Again, she described these as strobe lighting - their spirits flashed. Helena was blown away by what she witnessed. "This is huge, Irene. What is going on?" She continued to watch the events for a while. We didn't know what they were passing but found out quite soon. Whatever was happening, it was growing by the day. It was overwhelming, and everything was happening quickly.

The Process of Baptism

The Process

May 28th: The field was full of light beings. Helena knelt at the horse's water trough, observing her surroundings. Spirits of the deceased walked into the field, and nuns greeted them. The spirits knelt, put their heads in the water, and rose back up. Angels flew down, took them by their hands, and flew skywards and in through a doorway. The field was full of warrior-type angels, and another type flew down and collected the spirits. They had a 'process' or a 'system.'

Leaving Belle, she returned home, and I heard her sons playing in the background when Helena voice messaged, "Irene, I'm seeing something new here." For a moment, she wasn't sure what they were doing, but she witnessed an angel bending down and a pair of hands coming up toward the angel. The shimmering angel was hovering over the paddling pool and dipping something into it, which he lifted tenderly and passed to a nun who stood beside him. That nun passed it to the other nun that stood beside her. Helena continued to observe and said, "Irene, remember I told you they were passing something last night, but I didn't know what. Well, I think they are passing babies, toddlers, and small children. They are Irene! They are! They are lifting them up and dipping them in the water." It was early evening, and it was bright, so she continued to watch the process. Oval auras were aligned from the ground to the sky in a zig-zag shape. They passed the children to one another up the zig-zag staircase. At the top, they walked through a door where an angel stood and took the child through. We were amazed! We thought we had seen it all and had many experiences, yet there was still more.

Helena watched until it was time to make dinner for her children, and then later, she went to feed Belle. There were now *hundreds* of light beings and spirits there, and two queues of spirits entered from beyond the field. We were surprised by this. What started as one or two spirits coming to Helena had grown into hundreds. We were confused because Helena could never pray enough to release these numbers. But it was obvious as the days passed that she was being helped, that she was important in all of this, but something bigger was going on. There were now two doorways in the sky flanked by *two* giant light beings, and over the sea, she saw more.

She observed two giant beings on either side of her garden and our father's house. So, it was going on down the end of our road and in the sky outside our garden. She drank her tea as darkness descended, and we decided that Helena should ask Herou what was going on. I went to sleep in both wonder and disbelief. Who would believe any of this? No one – I hardly believed it myself, yet I knew my sister couldn't or wouldn't make this up. They were right when they said, 'In May, she would see and understand more.'

Spirit & Souls

May 29th: This was our sister Theresa's birthday, so I called Helena to talk about buying a cake and having it in her garden. The weather was beautiful, and her garden was a suntrap. Helena started to see the process going on in her house in miniature. The figures of the nuns were tiny, about the size of your thumb. It was strange, but nothing had been normal for months. It was as if she was shown inside what was going on outside and that the energetic light beings could expand or contract easily. I'm reminded of what Luther said to us months before, *"A spirit of light that shines bright, that's all you are you know Irene, micro, micro."* Helena said they were working day and night because she saw them passing long boxes to one another in her room the previous night.

At 10:00 am, Helena looked skywards, the doorways in the sky, and the hovering angels were still in their same positions, and the garden was full of angels. She noticed another doorway in the sky a good distance away over a local pub called The Brook. Helena recited her releasing prayer and realized that the 'process' started when she began to pray – they were waiting for her! She decided to contact Herou to see if he could tell us what was happening. So, after breakfast, she went into meditation. It took around ten minutes to connect, and it was 12:00 noon when she finished.

Helena: *Hello Herou.*

Herou: *Your fear now you must let go; we are now down there all around you, you know.*

Releasing spirits, we help you, it is true. We are down here now, all around you.

We pass spirit to one another, you see. We now help you and them with their journey.

From the airplanes to the heavenly, you see; we collect all of them, you see.

There are quite a lot of them for just you to get through,

So, we take care of a lot of them for you.

There's just too many for you to deal with on your own, you see.

They keep coming, they keep coming, they keep coming, you see.

There are quite a few, so we're helping. We are releasing with you, too.

Yes, children you did see yesterday, you know. We have to handle these children, you see.

They are baptized and cleansed in front of WE. It releases them to be free.

It releases them to be free to travel to where they need to be.

This is a process they have to go through.

Step into the new world they now have to do.

Cleansing our souls is something we all need to do.

This is the process for every soul to go through.

Helena: What is the difference between a spirit and a soul?

Herou: A spirit is you individually, the individual person that you are, you see. The soul is a combination of a lot of past lives. Past lives, my dear, of who you used to be. It's a collective of all the times you have been down on earth. But your spirit is your individual you. Who you are now, my dear, and you must be cleansed as soon as you reach up here. They didn't get to reach where they should be. So, the cleansing process we need to do is down on earth. This is what you're seeing with your own eyes, my dear. You have seen it appear in front of you. The process in which these lost souls have to go through.

Helena: *Why am I able to see this now, Herou?*

Herou: *You have stepped up, my dear, on this journey. There is going to be more that you will see. Throughout your journey, my dear, you will grow and grow, and we will release more information for you to know.*

Helena: *Am I the only person doing this on earth, or are there other people doing it?*

Herou: *There are people on Earth that release a few.*

But you, my dear, are different to thee; you release more because of who you used to be,

Yvonne, my dear in your soul, is she.

You have been chosen, my dear; this is the job for you.

The Holy Spirit is within side you. He has invested in you like He has invested in we.

You have been chosen to do this work; you see.

You stand up above the rest, my dear; this we want to make clear.

The spirit of SHE is within you.

Releasing souls is what she wanted to do.

Her spirit is within your soul, my dear.

Have I made myself clear?'

Is there anything else you need to know?

Is there anything else we can answer for you?

Helena: *I saw spirits through my third eye this morning; they looked like they were carrying boxes. What were they?'*

Herou: *They are supplies that are needed for we. We eat and drink just like Ye.*

Helena: *How long will I see you down on earth?*

Herou: *A few weeks, my dear. Release, release, release to we.*

Helena: *Anything you want to say to me?*

Herou: *Your life down on earth, you see, there will be lots more you will experience and see.*

We will release this to you when you are meant to know.

For now, my dear, we are all here.

To help you with the collection of spirit, my dear.

To release some of the pressure off you;

there are lots of souls we need to get through.

They are drawn to you from everywhere you see,

now we help you out, little Missy.

Goodbye, Helena, I need to let go,

we will talk again very soon, you know.

End of channel.

Later, Helena went to groom Belle and, surrounded by light beings, launched into prayer to keep the process going. At this time, Helena was constantly praying either in silence or out loud. Arriving home, she pulled into her front drive and closed the wooden gate behind her. In the lane, she noticed energy, but it was low to the ground. She focused harder and realized that it was the spirit energy of children who were around four or five years old. Helena asked them to move in, and they walked through her gate quite casually in groups of three and four. It was as if they were queuing for a carnival. Helena noticed the girl's clothes weren't modern. They wore frilly dresses and hats with ribbons as if they were from another time. This was the first time Helena had seen the full-form spirits of children. It was amazing, and when I think about this, I always feel like crying. I wonder why some children have been stuck here on earth. But Helena said they were just children talking with other children. They weren't upset or sad; they were just being kids. I think of all the parents who have lost children; their pain is unfathomable, but it seems that children are taken care of and go on. The ones who are stuck seem carefree. I would have loved to have seen this. I feel that I would have tried to throw my arms around them. Instead, I must listen to the description through a voice message and imagine this beautiful scene.

A Festival of Souls

May 30th: Helena messaged saying that she was so engrossed in watching TV the night before that she'd stopped praying. She glanced at her golden bowl and saw a steady stream of orbs moving toward it. "It's true, Irene, they were actually helping me!" Helena was delighted. It struck me once again that it took a long time for Helena to comprehend things. It could be days later when she absorbed information. There seemed to be more spirits being

111

released than prayers said by Helena. She said the energy that was thick in her cottage eased as they helped. Later that morning, Helena connected with Herou.

Dear You Can See

Helena: *Why are spirits stuck here on earth? Turmoil? Tragedy? Why are there so many?*

Herou: *You see, my dear, this is true.*

You do have people there to meet and greet you.

In these situations, you see, these spirits have all died in tragedy.

When they die, they cannot see who is there to take them away,

and then they are stuck, and they have to stay.

They are in shock when their spirit leaves their body,

and everything becomes a haze for they; they just can't see the way.

They are too busy looking at themselves, you see,

looking at their bodies at who they used to be.

Within those moments, it's very important for them to go through.

They waste this time by staring down at themselves, you see,

looking at who they used to be.

Within those moments, they need to go;

then they get trapped down there, you know.

Does this answer your question?

Helena: *Are all these tragedies that happen quickly? Deaths they are not prepared for?*

Herou: *Yes, my dear, this is true; it all depends on the individual you see.*

It's only moments where we can meet you and greet you,

and take you to where you need to be.

Within these moments, some focus on what it is that they do see.

Looking at themselves, you know, baffled at what just happened to them, you see.

The window and the opportunity for them to go through,

down on earth, you see, is momentary.

There is not a large window for us to come through.

Does that answer the question?

Helena: *Yes. Why does a person on earth need to do this work?*

Herou: *Good question, my dear; with this question, we cheer.*

To work with the spirit world, there is a process that you need to do,

you need to release your spirit and let it come through.

Only a specified amount of humans are selected, you see,

to work with us, you need to release to we.

But you, my dear, you're different, you know.

It's who you were on earth before, my dear.

You have worked with us before; you see,

your soul has a strong connection with we.

Yvonne, my dear, she is within you,

and this was something she wanted to do.

People release, but they only release a few.

A specific amount is all they have to do.

But we have all reconnected, and now we work with her,

and with you, my dear; yesterday, I have made this quite clear.

Helena*: You say that spirits are able to eat and drink. How can a vibration eat?*

Herou: *Hurray! You've got very interesting questions today!*

We are just like you; the physical body doesn't exist, you see.

We are still all spirits here on earth, you see.

And a spirit can eat and drink just like you.

There is another world down there on earth, you see,

a spirit can live on, just like ye.

We walk all around you every day, you know.

You can't see the unseen, you know.

We live on fruits and berries, you see; there are orchards down there, that you cannot see.

Natural foods that grow on earth, you see.

Helena: *And what do you drink?*

Herou*: Springs and rivers, there's water, you know!*

It's all around you down there, my dear.

It's a different dimension than ye, you know.

And we can survive for years, you know.

Helena: *Are these just recent spirits who have passed over? Or are they here for generations?*

Herou: *Generation, my dear, there is a good few,*

some who prevail and continue to roam,

The bigger amount of them, they want to come home.

There are some who will go and some who will stay;

there are some who just can't find their way.

We release the ones who want to go home,

The ones who are lost and continue to roam.

These ones are guided to you, you see?

Then there are ones that don't want to be free.

They're the ones who cause trouble to the earthlings, you see.

These will be the ones that we will help you with, you know,

ones that are stuck and who just don't want to go.

There are lots who cause trouble to earthlings, you see.

They live within their homes and annoy their families.

They attach to earthlings, you see,

They live among you all night and day.

A majority of them want to go,

A majority of them want to stay.

Helena: *Why do you have to handle the children's spirits here on earth?*

Herou: *The capabilities of they are not the same as the elders you see.*

Hands-on, we baptize them and cleanse them, you know.

We pass them and pass them and help them to go.

The adults, my dear, they can walk through.

The children we handle with care, you know.

We need to get them where they have to be.

Helena: *I see you work all around me. How come I can't capture your figures in a picture?*

Herou: *Pixels of light, that is all we are, you know.*

You're not picking up these pixels on your camera, you see.

In the future, my dear, you will capture a few.

Helena: *So, you will let me catch ones in the future? The ones I am allowed?*

Herou: *Only ones we want Earth to see!*

When that time comes, my dear, we will let you know.

We do want people to believe you in what you see and what you hear.

We will give you a little bit of evidence of this, my dear.

Till then, you will have to persevere.

We will alert you when the time is right, my dear,

exclusive images that are meant for just you. This will prevail for you.

Helena: *Are you collecting souls from the whole area?*

116

Herou: We are all around you, my dear,

they can see around this area so very clearly.

All around the vicinity of you;

they all gather the ones that want to go through.

It's like a festival of souls, you see,

we are truly, very, very busy.

Helena: *Is this the first time you have come to earth to do this?*

Herou: *We've done this through the centuries, my dear;*

every hundred years! We open up the doors from where we appear.

Helena: *Do you do this globally?*

Herou: *Yes, we do this too; it's not always just around you! (She giggled.)*

Is there anything else you would like to ask me?

Helena: *Is the way I see you now always going to be the way I see you, or is it going to change?*

Herou: *Another good question, Helena, you have just asked me.*

Over time, you will see more, my dear, in different ways we can appear!

This will be very exciting for you.

We tend to change in time as you go on,

the auras from what you see will get more strong.

So, don't worry about capturing a picture, my dear.

You will get pictures that are meant for you, my dear.

Irene's busy typing. We can see this.

She will document everything you know,

and we will give her exactly what it is she needs to know.

To do this book is very important to ye.

We will give you everything you need to go on, you see.

We are guiding you on the way; we want this to go.

Time will tell, and you will both see that all this is meant to be.

We will let the world know what we want them to know.

Now, my dear, I must leave you and go.

End of Channel

Helena: *Irene, I just saw four people walk through the door; actually, there are a good few.*

Panel: *We are the panel that represents you.*

Later, Helena sat in her garden observing events around her while simultaneously recording messages to me. *"I see a semicircle of women who are wearing aprons on their dresses, like maids in the old days. They tell me they're baptizing a baby. I see the baby naked with curly hair. They dip the baby in the water two to three times, and the angels carry the baby up to the door in the sky. They want me to see it. All of the heavenly angels are down on earth, and they are all helping. There are warrior angels, Knights of the Light, protective angels, nuns, priests, Maidens of the Sky, and baby angels."* Helena was pensive as she watched. *"We all think we are home, Irene, but we're not."* She wondered what else she should be doing. I suggested that she should try to draw them. *"They are a type of mist, Irene, so I can't draw them. How do you draw a cloud of mist? Imagine Irene, somebody blowing smoke rings; the smoke makes the shape of the rings. That is what these are like: outlines of people within a mist. I have to close my eyes and focus on all of them in order to get a closer look. I see a bit more detail with my eyes closed. When the angels bob in the sky and need to come down, I can see a faint line of mist fall behind them, like the aero plane trails. I'm seeing something else, Irene, in the distance. It looks like a giant light being. I'm going to keep watching this Irene, and I will talk to you later."*

Celestials Everywhere

May 31st: Helena messaged saying she did little releasing the night before, as the Celestials were working, so she took advantage and rested. During the night, she was woken repeatedly by frustrated spirits who bumped her bed. Losing her temper, she shouted at the spirits, ordering them to get out until morning. Her husband told her not to shout, but she was annoyed and needed sleep. I advised her, "Put yourself in their place, Helena; how would you feel if you were here for generations and wanted to go home?" She agreed with me. But I knew Helena was going through a lot, and *I* couldn't deal with what *she* was going through. It was easy for me to say when I was sleeping like a baby. She closed her eyes, and Herou connected quickly. He said whether they were helping her or not, she had her own target to reach, and she would go up a step in the spirit world's work.

The energy was still in her house, and she believed the spirits were not there in hundreds but thousands. At this stage, Helena was praying approximately four hours a day, continuing while doing daily chores. Going to the field, she walked towards the beach and saw the celestials in the sky over the estuary and sea. Later, she brought her child on a bike ride through Donabate. In a voice message, she said, "Irene, I'm baffled! They're not just in Portrane; they are over Donabate. What is going on? I thought they were helping me, but it looks like they are down here to collect spirits and lots of them. Have they always been here? Are they allowing me to see more daily? Are they here because of the pandemic? Is this a hundred-year thing? Because Irene, they are everywhere!"

The Collective Soul

June 1st: Was a very warm day, and Helena sat with her son James in the field, observing the surrounding activity. She witnessed a man sitting on a throne which moved toward her. He wore a cloak held together on the front with a clasp. The throne turned around and moved away. She didn't know who he was.

Later that day, sitting in her kitchen, a light arched doorway appeared outside her back door. Women were letting children in through this doorway. Helena's voice messaged, asking, *"Irene, if it's the children walking in, what is it they were passing? I'm just wondering, could it be the* soul? *I think they are collecting souls. Separating spirits and souls and making a collective soul. The collective soul of the spirit. Didn't Herou tell us we had a soul of all our spirits in the past? Do you think it could be the soul?"*

I don't know how Helena came to this profound understanding at that moment, unless that message was impressed upon her. It reminded me of something Luther had said to us in one of his many channels, *"Those heartfelt messages, they do all come from me."*

Helena began connecting with helper spirits in her house, who responded faintly at first. She closed her eyes and went travelling through tunnels where she met knights and warriors. Herou told her they were her *guides* and *guardians*. Again, this was *another introduction!*

Giant Light Beings

June 3rd: Was a warm but dull day. Helena drove to the field and saw a giant woman of light wearing a mob cap and an old-fashioned maid's dress. It was very distracting. When she entered the field, the king was seated on his throne, hands entwined on his lap. He bowed to her. The light beings were all in large form now. Helena tried to take photos and was frustrated that I couldn't see them; she desperately wanted someone other than herself to view them. It was my birthday, and later, I rested and meditated - all I saw was two pencils, a cup of tea, and a glass of wine. We cracked up laughing. I would be writing while drinking tea and wine. This described the next three years of my life!

June 4th and 5th: Helena went into meditation but saw no one, and it was uneventful. Everybody was busy; it appeared that collecting spirit was the priority, and Helena felt lost.

The Lagoon

June 6th: Helena closed her eyes, and immediately, her spirit went travelling. She saw the interior of a giant light transporter. It seemed to house one enormous cavern like an endless well, where water fell from the top like a waterfall and split into streams that flowed down the walls. Carved into the interior rocky walls were stairways and doors; she saw clouds as they led to the outside through those doors. Angels flew up, dropped something that looked like a ball of energy into the stream, and it flowed down, washing the negative energy that it had accumulated. All this within a giant light being! She heard the word 'lagoon.' There were rocky steps up to each doorway with angels and people walking around it. She believed they were putting souls into the stream of water. These giant beings seemed to be collection points for containing and cleansing thousands of souls.

June 7th: Helena messaged, saying someone woke her during the night by blowing on her face. She woke to see the light of a knight reflected on her ceiling. Scared, she woke Stephen, who told her she'd be OK and went back to sleep. Over to the right, there was another knight on horseback. His arm came through the ceiling and wall - they were passing things to one other. She was afraid but continued looking at the activity they *wanted her to see*. She said there was no way anybody would believe this. They were lime green flickering lights. They wore long gloves and passed something that looked like a long scroll. Helena found it difficult to explain what was going on. The only way I can visualise it is, it's as if an architect is designing a house on 3D software where you can turn the design model around and look at it from all angles. Well, her physical house was within this software model, and the light beings were working around her, and she could see it all. We were lost and had no one to turn to. I tried to confide in a couple of family members, but no one would listen. I understood what she was experiencing sounded ridiculous, but Helena was coherent, and when I felt momentarily that something didn't make sense, I would realize later that it did. I concentrated on writing down the channels and continued writing my children's stories to pass the lockdown. This left me with hundreds of voice messages to get through, and some had been deleted just for lack of phone storage. I wish I had written everything down day by day. In a channel with Herou, we learned about the Lagoon. Part of this message was deleted, but the second half goes on to talk about the well in the giant being.

The Lagoon

Herou: *It's like a stream, like a river, like a waterfall.*

The remainder of the souls they are taken here.

They place them in the water, you see; they

flow through to where they have to be.

The remainder of the souls go to where they have to go.

Helena: *So, it's a cleansing of your collective soul of who you used to be. What are you cleansing the souls of?*

Herou: *Negative energy that has been picked up.*

All the negative energy, all the pain, all the strain.

Things on earth that you did go through.

These have an impact on your soul, and this must be cleansed away.

Helena: *Where do they travel to when they are let go?*

Herou: *The energy is released.*

End of channel

My Dear You Can See

June 8th: In meditation, Helena was experiencing very little and was bored watching the process for weeks. The miraculous wasn't enough for Helena. Later, pulling into her driveway, she saw a cloud of energy dropping from the sky and coming toward her. It hovered in front of her. She closed her eyes, and the energy looked like a cloud, and within it was a man. He walked out and said, *"My dear, you can see."* A circle opened within the cloud, a door opened within the circle, and he was gone. This was *another introduction;* she would be seeing more.

Parallel Universe

June 9th: Helena woke to lots of activity in her room; light beings were flashing, and she heard running water. She tried to video, but they became quiet. A man sat in the corner of her bedroom as if overseeing things. Helena told him she wanted to send a video to Irene but knew as soon as she'd begun, she wouldn't capture anything. Then, a group of spirits walked straight up to her. She thought they'd disappear in front of her like a flow, but they didn't. She was scared as they were so close and real but realized they were the second shift of helper spirits. Her bed was bumped that night, so she asked her protectors to keep the frustrated spirits away. I advised her to get earplugs as she didn't want to hear them constantly ask for help. She'd reduced her praying over the previous days, doing only a couple of hours in the evening. She felt pressure in her head and knew someone wanted to connect – it was Herou.

Herou: *These are opposite parallel universes, and you are smack-bang in the middle of them. Helena, my dear, this is Herou. Yes, my sweet, you have been calling upon me. I have been watching you, you see. I have left you to get your bearings around the situation you see. Today, you are a little confused and down in yourself, too. The seen and the unseen, I did tell you.*

You are seeing things now that you haven't seen before; yes, these spirits can walk across a floor. They open the doors to this universe, you see. I'm channeling through to you way above up here; our connection is very clear. I am connected to them, too, who are around you. There are still lots of spirits all around you; they are desperate, waiting to get through.

You have to release a bit more for us; you eased a little on the releasing to us. You need to release more to us now, my sweet. I say this to you as I sit on my seat. We separate these spirits and souls, you see; we need to do this to bring them on through. The souls we gather and take away, we do this with you now, every day. Don't compromise, my dear, you see. You still need to release lots more to we.

What you're seeing and believing is very true; we are there giving you a hand and helping you. We are your friends now, my dear; this is true, generals and sergeants, you have met a few. They have met you in person and directed you; when you have come travelling too.

This is only the tip of the iceberg, you know. There is so much more you will experience and go through. This is still only really beginning for you. You're a clear seer now, my dear; you see the unseen. There is a lot more to be revealed to you: there will be so much more you will experience, too. Don't hesitate to call upon me if you really need to talk to me. You are not alone, my dear; we guide and protect you.

Helena: *What are the names of these universes?*

Herou: *My dear, we will eventually reveal this to you. Little by little, we will let you know; this is the way things have to go. Focus on releasing to us now, you see. I have made this very clear to you now, you know. My dear Helena, now I have to let you go. You are in safe hands, my sweet; no harm will ever come to you.*

You are very well protected from all of us; we protect you and your family. Things will unwind in time, you see. Your journey is long, my dear; we will keep it in gear. Fast forward to this: we cannot do; just keep one foot ahead of another, that is all you have to do.

Walk along and keep steady; in time, you will see, there's more of the unseen you will see. Dearest thanks, Helena, Dearest thanks to you.

We are there giving you a hand and helping you, too;

this you believe is true.

End of channel.

Someone knocked on her front door, so she disconnected. She came back to the couch, and the pressure in her head was strong, so she closed her eyes. A man spoke to her, but first, he knelt in front of her, put his hand on his knee, and bowed to Helena. Hank snored in the background.

War Veteran: *Herou asked me to speak to you; I am a war veteran, you see. I sit on my chair. Can you see me in front of you, my dear?*

Helena: *Yes, I can.*

Man: *We are from a parallel universe, you see. (Helena couldn't pronounce parallel; she tried to say it 4-5 times.)*

We are the beings you see.

We work together up here in unity.

We give service to the spirits and souls as well too.

We work all around you.

We work from up here, from within this hemisphere.

We are guides and guardians to you.

We all work for The Almighty, too.

We combine our strengths up here, you see.

We live in peace and unity.

Were like a transatlantic airline, you see.

We combine our strengths in unity.

Our passengers are brought directly to where they need to go,

and this is the work we do, you know.

Transport them to the destination where they need to go.

Do you understand now what it is that we do?

That is my way of trying to describe it to you.

We must retreat, my dear, and go,

we will talk to you again soon, you know.

End of channel.

The Process of Soul Removal

The Gathering

That evening, as Helena drove to the field, large oval auras lined both sides of the road. One floated directly across her, and she was annoyed by the distraction until she realized it was on purpose - they *wanted* her to take notice. The ovals contained a variety of light beings; some were females dressed like old-fashioned maids with mob caps and aprons. They held their hands in the prayer position and bowed to Helena. It became too much for Helena, and she cried. They bowed to her, and through her tears, she bowed back. They seemed to reassure her that she would be okay. In the previous weeks, the spiritual activity had strengthened. Angels, nuns, lost souls, and numerous other light beings were working around her. She saw giant beings, knights, and horsemen. She heard spirits cry for help, others bumped her bed, while spirit workers came through her bedroom. I tried to calm her by telling her that the world would love to see something spiritual, even if it was just an angel. She was lucky she got to see all of heaven. She wondered if other mediums saw anything like this and said she would ask Herou. She couldn't get this 'medium business' out of her head. It didn't matter how many times they told her she was different – that Yvonne Beauvais was in her soul- it just did *not* get through. Helena just wanted to be a medium.

June 10th: Helena voice messaged saying that the previous night in her garden, she was shown a woman sitting on a chair, and on her knee was an open book. A male spirit knelt in front of the woman who placed her hands lovingly on his shoulders as she read from it. The spirit kissed its pages, then knelt, and his head was dipped into water three times. Helena thought the book was the Bible. I wondered if it was the book of his life. Whichever book it was, it had been shown to her in visions before *as an introduction.* She was right when she thought the book was *significant.* This morning, she

127

once again watched a seated woman perform the same routine. Helena walked towards her to get a closer look. The woman was dressed like a maid, wearing an apron and mob cap. She was very ladylike in her movements - when she sat, she neatly tucked her dress under her.

In the afternoon, Helena went to Belle, and it seemed quiet for a moment; she couldn't see anybody, and then suddenly, a light door opened right in front of her! It was intended for Helena to see it. As usual, people exited the door and walked to the right and left like a curtain call. Helena was told, '*We gather here to release souls, my dear.*' The woman walked to a chair and sat down. There were men in the gathering also. Helena started to pray, and a female spirit walked over to the seated lady. The spirit knelt, and the woman placed a hand on the back of her head and guided her head into a vessel; when the spirit rose, Helena saw a beautiful glow; she said it was like the glow of Patrick Swayze's spirit leaving his body in the movie *Ghost*. It was a beautiful iridescent and glowing **purple** light. They lifted the glowing light and passed it to an angel, who took it away in a pot-like vessel about the size of a tennis ball. Then she witnessed the process again, but she saw it more clearly this time. This time, a man knelt before the seated woman. Helena noticed that when he rose, his mouth was open and exhaling a flow of glowing purple energy. The people collected and passed this energy to one another, then handed it to an angel. "*Irene, the energy poured out of his mouth, gathering and changing to a ball of light. Just a glowing ball of purple light. It is the soul. The soul is within the spirit, and when it's released, it is a beautiful light that changes into a ball of light. The angels then take it away. It's a beautiful, gentle, and loving experience.*" Helena was in awe while I felt the hairs stand up all over my body.

Later at home, Helena was shown a similar scene and voice messaged. She was crying as she whispered; she didn't want her children to hear. In a vision, she saw women sitting in a circle inside her children's bedroom. In the center was water, and women helped children into the water. The children stepped out of the water and walked over to a seated woman. They leaned over quite casually and exhaled their soul into a vessel. Helena saw the children wrap their arms around the woman's neck, embracing her, and then they walked through a light door. The children were relaxed and happy. This continued for about five or six children so that Helena could really see. It was so beautiful that Helena could not hold back her tears. "It's precious, Irene. It's so beautiful." I couldn't hold back my own tears when I heard the emotion in Helena's voice.

Babies

June 11th: The previous night Helena woke to a sparkling atmosphere over her bed. Many people were in auras; they didn't mind her looking at them, and she was no longer afraid. They moved across her bedroom and up to the ceiling, where they passed stuff to each other. She let them go about their business. A knight sat in the corner of her room. He'd get up, walk around the chair, and sit back down repeatedly. Helena joked that she didn't blame him because her bedroom was tiny. He wore a knee-length leather skirt with a belt and a sword, and his boots came high up on his legs. Images of Hamlet came to my mind. Helena had watched Ophelia on Netflix and agreed the attire was the same. She could hear the odd spirit plead, "Help me." Helena knew the knight was guarding her.

Later, with Belle, Helena sat at the stable door and looked out - a door opened in front of her, and she saw children sliding down a slide as if in a playground. She saw a woman lift a toddler from under his arms, and it looked like she gave him a kiss. She put him down, and with a jug, poured water over his head. She bent down and put her face very close to his face and sucked the soul out of his mouth. Then, she passed it into a vessel herself. Another woman lifted a baby and showed Helena the baby, which she cradled in her arms and nuzzled down to its face. She then got a jug and poured water over the baby's head. Then with her hand, she gently moved the bottom of the baby's chin down until its mouth was open and put her mouth over its mouth and sucked the soul out, thus displaying the process for babies.

Helena noticed that the four doors in the sky stayed in the same position, and she knew their location. That evening, Helena contacted Herou.

Helena: *Do children get lost?*

Herou: *Children can get lost. All spirits can get lost, even children.*

Children do get lost, too; they live in a dimension all around you.

They are dense with their souls attached to them; you see,

we release the souls to set them free.

They live on earth in the dimension, a dimension there with you;

and we release them, and we take them through.

Helena: *Are they sad, or are they happy?*

Herou: *That's an awkward question for me.*

Happiness can be defined in many ways, my dear; they feel despair.

They know they are not complete, and they know they are not where they have to be, but they do live a happy life down there.

Yes, in sadness they can be, they know they are not up here with we.

Helena: *Who cares for them?*

Herou: *There are carers of thee; it's like adoption, you see.*

Fostering beings, there are down there a few.

They do care for the children, you know.

They look after them just like your parents did for you;

they care and feed and dress them, too.

Different generations they live among you.

We return and take them away; some of them don't come with us; they stay.

Helena: *Do they remember their families?*

Herou: *Of course, they do! They get reunited with their families in time, you see.*

Just like what you are doing here with me!

We communicate in this universe, my dear! (It was a joke, and Helena laughed.)

It's no different, really, to down there.

Helena: *What feeds the soul?*

Herou: *The soul feeds on the experiences you have down there.*

In your time down there, you see.

Experiences you have gone through.

All the knowledge you have learned along the way.

It feeds on the information you have learned down there.

This is collected and taken back up here to we.

It's like a book, a book of knowledge to we.

It's full of information for we. Like a microchip from Earth, you see.

Helena: *What darkens the soul?*

Herou: *It's the badness of the earth, my dear, what you have experienced down there. All the hate, all the evil you see,*

this seeps into the soul, you see.

Helena: *What happens to these souls?*

Herou: *They are taken to a different timeline, my dear;*

where it is very dark, and within the darkness, they disappear.

End of Channel.

Honors and Resurrections

Books

June 14th: Helena continued to pray and heard individual spirits ask for help; some talked amongst themselves. She heard one say, "We need the water." Now, *two* knights were in her room, one on either side of her bed. There was lots of activity. Helena thought there was much more going on than we knew about, and she was right again.

June 15th: In her garden, a nun dressed like Mother Teresa, wearing a veil that flowed long into her dress, bowed to Helena. The nun sat on a chair, and a child walked up to her, followed by a priest. He put his hands together, bowed to Helena, then got down on his hands and knees and kissed the ground in front of the girl. He stood up and worked on the girl who exhaled her soul into the vessel. The child then walked through a light door.

Helena had begun hearing lost spirits *outside* pleading with her to help them. They cried out, "Help me! Help me! I want to go home!" It sounded as if crowds were in the fields beyond, waiting to be released. Off in the distance, she believed she heard one shout, *"O holiest of girls, hello!"* Then another, *"Help us, come on? Send us home! Come on, let us go!"* It was as if what Herou said was true – it was 'a festival of souls', and they called upon the holy girl to set them free.

In the afternoon, Helena, in meditation, searched for Herou. The colours of the tunnels were different, and she was directed somewhere new, finding herself in a new building. She was greeted by a knight who ran his hands along a wooden shelf and found a set of keys. He opened a door and was met by a woman who held a book and flicked through the pages - Helena heard the world *scriptures.*

The woman spoke.

Books of knowledge, my dear.

Everything is recorded and written down here, you see;

books of information for we.

Recorded all over history, all the lives of people, and who they used to be.

Everything is documented, my dear; we record it all and keep it here.

Every last word of everyone's experience you see it's like one large library.

We revise everything you see about the world and how it has changed over the centuries.

Every single person you have been down on earth, my dear;

this building is just made for this here.

We have more than just the archives up here.

Now we go through, there is something else I want to show you.

Stairways down to the lower basement, you see.

This is where the book of YOU will be. She pushed another door open.

My dear, we will show you here.

They were showing her just how big the place was. Helena said, *"The interior of this building was like a castle, and through every door, there was another room and winding staircases."* The woman said, "This building is much bigger than the Spiritual Archives," (Which Helena had been shown before, but I omitted from this book). The halls were lined with millions of books and paperwork.

The woman ran her hands along them, took one out, and, blowing the dust off it, said, *"All the information recorded of spirits and souls. All our experiences here on earth, past, present, and future of all generations, are recorded and kept here. What goes on in the world? What changes in the world over the centuries, they revise it."*

Helena then remembered having a vision of a religious book the previous night; it reminded her of the Book of Kells. This was *another important introduction* of what was to come.

15:50 pm: Helena voice messaged and explained what was happening as it was happening! *"I'm in my garden, and a big door has opened in front of me; behind the door, curtains are opening. A group of nuns are walking out to the left and right, and a priest and head nun are coming out and standing to the side. The nun is like a Mother Superior."*

Then Helena's spirit went flying through the door into a cathedral; she then flew outside and upward, viewing its exterior. It had side steps leading into the surrounding gardens where nuns walked in groups. A man, possibly a priest, was in a bell tower tolling a bell – she heard ding, ding, ding. Nuns opened and closed the windows, showing features of the cathedral *they wanted her to see.* Back inside, a bishop knelt in front of an altar, looked toward Helena, and bowed - nuns stood around him. He then sat on a raised cathedra as the nuns looked up at him. He stood up and sat down a few times, showing himself to Helena. Helena got the impression that this was something to do with Yvonne Beauvais. Opening her eyes and looking skywards, she saw the bishop on his cathedra and the nuns on either side of him. They all bowed, and the sky around them sparkled. We didn't know it then, but they were preparing a ceremony to honor Yvonne Beauvais.

19:34 pm that evening, Helena went horse-riding. She messaged, "Irene, I'm here on the beach beside Kelly's field and letting Belle eat grass. I've just been surrounded by nuns who said, *"Yvonne Beauvais, we show ourselves to you, Mother Superior."* Then something more astonishing happened. Helena's voice was shaking as she spoke on the recording; she was trying to figure out what she was seeing and how to explain it. I am going to write this word for word as it's on the WhatsApp recording.

Helena: *They are after getting a crucifix, Irene; this is mental; they are after getting a crucifix, and there were a few of them; they laid down the crucifix. Somebody lay down on the crucifix as if they were going to crucify him. They are carrying the crucifix back in. Em, I think they were showing Jesus being crucified on the cross. Then they poured water on the end of it... at the end of the cross, and they got up and walked away, but I heard, "He died and rose again," and basically, you are living again. Now, they are all walking away into the distance. Holy crap Irene, this is mental. It's like you gave yourself to Jesus, and now He is returning the favor to you. You are back down on this earth once more, just like He. (Her voice was shaking) I'm a bit emotional now, I have to say, but yeah, that's just after happening, Irene."*

I received a voice message twenty minutes later. Helena was speaking frantically.

Helena: *Right, I am in Kelly's field. I'm being followed by nuns and priests. I can only ride Belle on Kelly's land because I can't ride her on the beach as the tide is in. There were priests seated on thrones, so I closed my eyes to see if I could connect with them. Then, the next minute, I saw hundreds, and I mean hundreds of nuns, and it was like I was being fast-forwarded through the crowd of nuns. They had formed a walkway on either side of me, and I was walking through them, and all the nuns were going by me, going by me, going by me, which brought me straight through big doors into a huge cathedral, bigger than a cathedral because they were up on balconies to the right and left. As I walked up the aisle, every single nun stood up, and I mean hundreds of them, standing up from their seats and applauding. I kept on going by them, and they continued to clap. Then, a door opened, and behind it was a bishop holding a crozier; he wore a large gold object around his neck. He then lit up, and curtains closed around him. I turned around, and the congregation of nuns continued to clap. So, it's like the heavens are applauding and acknowledging Yvonne Beauvais today, saying, "You are her! You are her! They are saying, "You live again! You live again!"*

June 15th: At 20:52 pm, I received another message from Helena, her voice was shaking.

Helena: *I'm back in the field, and they have done it again. They came out with the crucifix, put it on the ground, and someone lay on it. Then they poured water over the person and lifted it up, turning it around to face me. Bishops and other clergy are standing right in front of me. Irene, you should hear all the spirits crying out for help. All I can hear is, "Help! Help! Help!" They are in the background shouting with force. Then, I closed my eyes to look through my third eye to see if I could connect, and the same thing happened again. They came rushing out with a crucifix, put it on the ground, and the person looked like a monk or something, and when he lay down on it, they raised it up again. So, I saw the crucifix vision three times …pause… they poured water over the top of the crucifix…pause… are they cleansing the body? It's like they are pouring water over him, and he is lifting his head up and looking at me while he is lying down on his crucifix, and they are pouring water over him like holy water. I think it's a cleansing. I don't know. I don't know. But then, after that, do you know the crucifix that you can make out of straw? Do you know the ones that have the square in the middle? (St. Brigid's cross) they had one of them, and all the nuns were standing in front of me, passing one of them to each other and bowing to me. It reminds me of Knock (*A place of pilgrimage in Ireland where Our Lady is said to have appeared.) There is a major holy event going on down here, Irene. There is a lot going on.*

That evening, the visions continued. Overwhelmed, Helena narrated the description of events while simultaneously trying to comprehend them. From what I heard; it sounded like her surroundings were thronged with people. The celestials were telling Helena (Yvonne Beauvais) that she had risen from the dead like Jesus. I felt the blood draining from my body like I was going to get sick. I was trembling, and two minutes later, Helena voice messaged, explaining what was happening *as* it was happening. Again, she was frantically trying to understand the vision they were showing her.

Helena: *They slid it into a tomb and closed the tomb door, but when I see the door reopen, a bright light is coming out, and then angels are flying out of the doors…where the cross, (she exhaled) Ah man! It's mad! I'm trying to watch what they are doing with the crucifix. They are just tilting it up and down, tilting it up and down, washing it, putting it in a tomb, taking it out of the tomb. They took it out of the tomb, and a bright light came out. Now they are tilting it again, tilting it again, and I don't know if they are trying to say, you rise again, you rose again, you know… I don't know! They just seem to be repeating this. Am I not getting it? I know what I heard the first time it was done, but they just keep doing it. Lying down on the crucifix, dragging the crucifix in, like a tomb… closing doors. Doors reopen, light comes out, there's an angel, yeah, there's the bright light coming out again! Now it's like someone on a throne coming out. Ah, I don't know. I'm getting a bit lost now, Irene. There is so much going on. It's like I open my third eye; there is stuff going on. I open my eyes, and there is stuff going on. They are all around. They are just everywhere."*

Helena informed me in the following text that they kissed him on the head. Him? Who? Believe it or not, this was happening so fast that we couldn't understand what was happening or what they were trying to say. She was shown so much in a short period of time; it's only as I played the audio repeatedly that I think I understand what was happening. To me, the celestials were telling Helena that Yvonne Beauvais had come back on earth like Jesus Christ to save these souls, and just like Jesus Christ, she had risen again. The many cries Helena heard were the spirits waiting to be released. Jesus had given Yvonne her wish to save souls. But in the second vision, Helena saw a *man* on a crucifix, a tomb, then a light coming out of the tomb with angels, and a man on the throne being kissed on the head. This sounded like a representation of the Resurrection of Jesus. Were they just showing her His image to get their point across about Yvonne being reincarnated through Helena? Or was this *another introduction* of what was to come? Was Jesus coming back, too? At that time, we didn't know, but we soon found out.

Selection of Angels

June 17th: Helena continued to hear the cries of people - one shouted, *"Christ will help you!"*

At 15:17 pm, she closed her eyes and was shown a building within a walled city like Carcassonne in France. There were thousands of people charging through the opening of the wall. The wall was so thick; the opening was like a short tunnel where they ran through and congregated on the other side in a very large courtyard - the people crammed in. As they pushed their way forward to the front of the courtyard, a man sat at quite a height on a throne. Beneath him was a wooden structure, and a large crucifix was protruding from it, which lay horizontally over their heads. The crowds continued to swarm in. The courtyard was shaped like a large church but without a roof. Embedded in the high walls surrounding the courtyard were alcoves, and within each alcove sat a clergyman on a smaller throne who looked down on the crowds below.

After seeing this vision, she went to the field where the celestials were working. Helena believed that as the masses were baptized and the process of soul removal had happened, the people left the earthly dimension and arrived in the courtyard on the 'other side.' They congregated in front of this man with the hierarchy of clergy around him in the courtyard.

Helena was then called to our dad's house as our sister Theresa, a diabetic, had gone into a hypo. Helena rushed to her, gave her honey, and held her until she came through. As Helena waited, she was shown a similar scene as her previous visions. Women sat in a circle, and within it was a man on a crucifix, which lay flat on the ground. A woman held in her hand a vessel like the priests use in mass to flick holy water on the congregation. The woman walked around the crucifix and flicked the water on the man from the toes to the head. Then the person sat up, and she put a cloth around his eyes, tied it around his head, and the man lay down again.

17:50 pm: At home, Helena was shown the city again. There were structures like small bell towers on top of the city walls, and in these structures, maidens stood. They held basins of water, and as the spirits ran into the courtyard, they poured water over their heads. Its layout was like Disneyland, one big walled city; churches, buildings, roadways, and courtyards were within it. People were walking throughout, going in different directions. Within its walls lay a large building with lots of empty space around it, and behind it was an enormous church. Through the crowds, Helena saw four people carrying a person on a stretcher. They placed it on a raised walkway (like a catwalk), which priests and nuns walked onto from the steps of the building so the whole crowd could see. The clergy poured water and ran their hands over the body. Helena's viewpoint became a bird's eye view, and she looked straight down on the body. As the water flowed off the person, she saw the most beautiful glowing light from which rose an angel who flew to the top of the building, looked down, and waved to the crowd before going through a door in the building. Helena was upset and said, "I feel like crying because I don't know what's going on, but I think they're showing a human spirit being released, blessed, and becoming an angel." Minutes later, her question was answered. I noticed they were good teachers. Little by little, they showed her things by repeating the process. A priest flanked by nuns walked down the steps into the crowd; with arms outstretched, he picked up a child dressed in white and walked through the archway to the other side. Laying the child on the stretcher, they ran their hands and poured water over its body, which then glowed, transforming it into an angel. They continued picking people and children from the crowd.

Later, in the field surrounded by clergy, she was once again shown a vision of angel selection. This time, the clergy held a box which they opened with a key. Inside it, she believed she saw *something like* the Sacred Heart – although she couldn't be sure what it was.

The circular openings in the sky that Helena witnessed for weeks seemed electrically charged. When there was movement, the circumference of the openings took on a jagged edge as if something electrical was happening. They showed Helena today that these energetic circles were the entrances of a giant floating light church.

Exodus

The Clergy in Her Room

June 18th: A priest within his aura stood outside Helena's back door the previous night. He bowed to her, and Helena bowed back. She made me laugh by saying she went over to the window and pulled the curtains. She was too scared to see spirits outside at night. She went to bed at 1:00 am and found him standing in her bedroom; he continued bowing. An energetic tunnel opened behind him; the interior of this tunnel looked like a corridor into a castle - he turned and walked through. A river of energy flowed from her sitting room and followed him through the tunnel. He was leading the spirit's home.

While this went on, she continued to see knights coming in and out of her bedroom carrying on with their work. At four am, she woke and voice messaged, "Irene, you are not going to believe this. There's a nun standing here wearing a veil with a white strip across her forehead and a black habit." More energy came flowing through her bedroom, pushing her door further open and following the nun through the tunnel.

She wondered why everyone was appearing in her house. She was nervous but reminded herself that they were heavenly beings. Later in the field, she watched the church hover with its doors open while thousands of people ran through. Nuns poured water over them, then closed the doors until the nuns refilled the buckets to pour over the next crowd. She was shown it happening in different doorways, displaying the church's size and that it had always been there. They had just been showing her parts of it over time. But it hovered over the whole peninsula and maybe even further away because there was an entrance everywhere Helena looked. She drove to Donabate to take money from the ATM and voice messaged, "They told me I was *'just to release souls,* but that's Yvonne's wish, not mine. I want to be a medium.'' Even at that stage, Helena thought she should get what she would like. Helena really didn't comprehend any of this.

The Endless Depth

June 19th - The pressure in Helena's head was strong as she was shown a vision of an endless circular well, like the interior of a large Round Tower. She felt it was a deep cavern where they dumped negative energies or negative spirits. There were staircases scattered around the edges that led to doors on top. Various people and knights walked on these staircases and exited the doors that were sealed shut behind them. The doors blended into the walls as water flowed down them. It looked like the endless depth that Luther described to us in our first channel. Spirit energy flew around and around inside, unable to get out - they were trapped!

Our Lady

June 21st: Helena, while in meditation, had a visitation from the Blessed Virgin; she saw her as a real person, *not* a light being. Our Lady radiated a beautiful blue that Helena had never seen before and wore a small gold crown like a tiara. Our Lady didn't stay long and said nothing.

Heavenly Transporters

June 22nd: The river of energy continued to rush through her bedroom and out through a tunnel. Along this river of energy, knights rode on horseback. She closed her eyes and had a vision of people running through a forest and scattering everywhere while the horsemen rounded them up like sheep. She recorded while in meditation, asking spirit workers some questions.

Helena: *Why are the horsemen chasing the people?*

Spirit: *They have to help them through.*

Helena: *Why are they calling me holy Girl?* .

143

Spirit: *You are a holy girl.*

Helena: *What makes me a holy girl?*

Spirit: *God is within you.*

Helena: *Is Yvonne Beauvais in my soul?*

Spirit: *Of course she is! Why do you sleep so long?*

Helena: *I am human.*

Helena's prayers became like a chant, and what was one tunnel had turned into three. Her visions showed that there were not thousands of spirits running but millions. The horsemen gathered them, the celestials released their souls, and when Helena prayed, a portal opened, and they flew through to the next world. Her house was alive with spirit energy, and as she prayed, she watched it exit the tunnel. This continued day and night, and Helena was very tired; it was wearing her down. She heard the helper spirits say to the deceased, "Walk through. Move on. Walk through. Move on." The spirits were corralled like sheep. She overheard one say, "Holy people take your souls." "Why," asked another. One responded, "Only the holy get through."

Helena drew pictures of the crowds, spending hours drawing little circles for heads to show me just how many were running through. When I saw the pictures, it really hit me that she was clearly SEEING this. We believed the spiritual armies had come down weeks before, traveled over the world in some dimension, and fought darkness to save souls.

Later, she messaged and said she felt it might be coming to an end. The three tunnels had become one large tunnel, and kings were now riding through as if the armies had collected enough and were leaving. When she closed her eyes, the tunnel was a spinning vortex of red energy that moved extremely fast, and as the river of spirit flowed in, it was sucked through at massive speed. She saw horsemen coming back out of a tunnel that opened beside the other one as if they were collecting the last of the people.

Helena asked the spirit helpers what was going on.

Helpers: *They are collecting them and going through them. They are collecting them and going through them.*

Helena: *How long is this going on for?*

Helpers: *They are going home. Yes, they have to go through you. Now we are flying through in you. Time to go home. All the people trust you. But Christ, He is gone into time. This house is bringing us home and all your body. We are going through until Sunday. You will see it close. Christ wants you to take them home. He is your friend. A person we go through. We told you, a person, you are everything. You are safe.*

Later, Helena went to the field and sent me a voice message. She was excited! *"Irene, they are all marching along the Burrow Rd. Then they started to march through me. Angels are at my feet; there is a lot of white light at my feet. I felt pain in my feet."*

In the distance, Helena described giant light beings that opened their chests, and the spirits of people poured out as a river of energy. They had collected millions of spirits and brought them to Helena. As the people poured out onto the ground, the horsemen charged around the spirits, corralled them into crowds, and drove them to the area where Helena was. Their collective energy formed a river of energy, and it flowed through the light doorway that was appearing in front of her feet. Baby angels flew around Helena's feet, and there was havoc and mayhem. People shouted, "Take me! Take me! Let me go!" Helena couldn't bear listening to them. She was distraught, saying she couldn't wait until Sunday when they would finish. As the spirits ran up the road, horsemen flanked them while large Maidens of the Sky stood pouring water over them. Above the maidens, large oval auras bobbed along either side of the road. Within these oval auras were high-ranking clergy, who sat and watched the progress, like dignitaries on high benches watching a parade pass by. Helena drew this for me, and the clergy in the ovals reminded me of the clergy in the courtyard alcoves on the other side.

Saints

June 24th: Helena was once again shown the tunnel of rotating red energy followed by the vision of people entering the walled city. On top of the wall, men stood pouring water onto the crowds. When the spirits ran through the archway, there was a fork in the road and a building in the middle, and they ran left and right, scattering everywhere. There was nothing modern about this city, which had cobblestone-type houses with apex roofs. A lot of these houses were tall and terraced and met the height of the city wall. The roads could be made of cobblestones or dirt, but she couldn't see them because of the crowds. She did see a church in the middle of this large city. People waved and greeted the new arrivals from the house windows, pouring water over them as they ran through the streets. Helena was shown this over and over again. We believed this was home to some of the spirits - that they all have different homes to go to. The Gardens of God are different; angel Thomas told us that some of the streets were paved with gold. It seems that the afterlife is a complex place. To get a sense of the size of this city and its many entrances, one of the giant transporter beings had to bend down to go through the tunnel entrance, which had old wooden doors with metalwork.

Then Helena was guided to fly *through* the tunnel of energy, which rotated like a 'twister,' and she noticed that water flowed through it this time. Within the tunnel were doorways that people exited. Her impression was that these doors were entrances into different worlds. She also passed through grids within the tunnel, and as everyone exited the tunnels, two knights greeted them. It's worth noting that every tunnel that Helena flew through was guarded by a man seated at its entrance and guarded at its exit by knights. After this, Helena went into her bedroom to ask the worker spirits what would happen to us when all this was finished; she desperately wanted this part to be over. At this stage, I couldn't blame her. She wasn't prepared for who would answer her. This continued to shock us.

Helena: *Will I let the world know God exists?*

Voice*: Yes, you will. Yes, you will do this.*

Helena: *Will the world believe?*

Voice: *You will let them know. Yes, the world will know.*

Helena: *Who is this that I am talking to?*

Saint Andrew: *Saint Andrew. We thank you for this. Christ has already gone through with all the saints back to heaven. God chose you. He trusts you.*

She asked for a name, and she believed she heard Bishop Lucifer. She thought he might be one of the Community of the Heavenly. Later, she went horse riding on the beach and described what she saw as MAGNIFICENT. As she rode, the energy flowed to her like rain. Across the sea, she saw giant light beings walking toward her on the water; they came from everywhere. At their feet rode thousands of light beings: horsemen, knights, soldiers, warriors, and kings from all armies throughout the centuries. As they rode, their hooves kicked up the water behind them, splashing it in the air. Spirits were released from both the knights and the giant light beings. She said, "They look like they're riding on rays of sunlight." The scene sounded like something from a movie. Around her, spirits chanted,

"Holy girl, get us through.

Holy girl, get us through.

Holy girl, help us through to the holy worlds."

More Heavenly Beings

June 25th: Helena travelled through long and vast tunnels. She heard a voice say, '*Yes, they are vast.*' Three images flashed in front of her. The first was the Sacred Heart - it was red with a gold light on top; the second was the bottom of a brown robe over bare feet. She believed it was Jesus. She saw this image as a real person, *not* a light being. The third was a map on white paper. The significance of the map has not been revealed to us yet. However, one day, Helena picked up a white Bible in my aunt's house and opened it. A map inside resonated with her as if she had seen it before. So maybe it could have been a biblical map that she was shown. These visions were once again *an introduction*. She asked questions as she heard spirit voices in the tunnel, although she did not know who was speaking to her.

Helena: *How many worlds are there?*

Voice: *Thousands! You are going through our worlds.*

Helena: *All the worlds seem to be made of stone and bricks.*

Spirit: *Every world but this. All the worlds look like this.*

Helena: *There are people standing at every tunnel doorway.*

Voice: *Yes, this is true. They guard them mostly. They help us go through.*

Helena: *Why am I always seeing water?*

Voice: *Water helps us travel. It makes the city hard. So, we can transport. It hardens the world. She heard someone say, "Shut up!"*

Helena: *Why are they all going through me?*

Voice: *You were chosen. Christ knew that you would help Him help us.*

Helena: *I see big castles in the sky and giant people. How will they get back? Are they going to come through me?*

Voice: *No, they go to another world. They help us from heaven. They help us go through. They go back to God. They go back to He.*

Helena: *I see armies, and they flow through to me. Why? To get to earth?*

Voice: *Yes, to get on earth. Yes, exactly; they are Godly helpers from all over the world. They round us up basically and help us from this world.*

Helena: *What are these giant beings? What are their names?*

Voice*: They are helpers that march through heaven; they are heavenly monsters.*

Helena: *They told us the armies are here to fight for the light. Are they fighting evil here on earth to save you?*

Voice: *They help us from evil on this earth. It's all around. Yes, that is all true. Satan, exactly, is in this world too. They help us fight him. They fight for us. They are fighting all over the world. They are helpers to help us get home.*

Next, she's shown large Maidens of the Sky standing in a line pouring water over spirits as they ran. Behind them stood even larger maidens, who blew spirits from their mouths that flowed into the running crowd and into this river of energy. Helena drew this for me. Later, she went to the field where the activity continued, and the crowds were chanting:

"Take us through, holy Girl; take us to all our worlds.

Take us through, holy Girl; take us to all our worlds."

Helena said "It's mental and amazing! How are we going to describe this? It is spectacular! It's like you're on a trip, but it's awesome. They are everywhere around me." She went home and lay down. They showed her a closer image of the 'monsters' they *wanted* her to see them. These looked like giant men, and the torsos of these giants were castles. Over the previous weeks, Helena witnessed castle entrances in the sky and church entrances, which confused me as I wasn't sure which she was seeing. But with a closer image of these giant transporter beings, I realized she was seeing both. She drew them out for me quite clearly. The men could detach and blend into the castle like it was a backpack they clicked into. The stomach area was an entrance. "This is crazy, Irene. It's like the whole castle is rock, and he can click in and out of it. He is swaying to the right and left, and water flows out of its windows. It's him making the castle tilt. He is turning to the left and right and tilting to show me all the door entrances into the castle. I was only seeing each entrance individually. I thought these smaller castles were floating in the air. Now I see, it is the torso of a light being on legs, a heavenly transporter being."

She was then shown a close-up view of a knight sitting on the castle-man's seat as if he was directing this being. The knight got up to show Helena his seat, which was an entrance into the castle. It was like something out of a fantasy movie. The knight made a point of showing Helena a light under his seat. A gold light like some sort of crystal. Helena only told me then that all these knights and armies had this piece of crystal light. (Everybody had a piece of light!). She drew a picture of a sword for me, and a crystal was in the centre of its handle. All these armies and monster beings were the colour of ice—iced blue like an ice cube. The knight took this gold crystal and put it in the head of the monster being, allowing the castle to unlock and let spirits flow out. She released all evening and was shown once again the monster being long enough for her to draw it. Her drawing was very detailed. Maybe a small book with these drawings will be published in the future. Helena's prayer had become more like a chant.

Pegasus

Direct transcript of what Helena witnessed at 8:30 pm later that evening. She can be heard whimpering on this audio.

Helena: *Oh, Irene, I'm in tears. I'm in tears; you won't believe what's in front of me. It's just a dream, Pegasus - flying horses. There are horsemen on the Pegasus, and they are flying and dropping down through the clouds. They are flying towards me, and their riders are getting the horses to bow to me. They have one leg extended and the other bent underneath them. So, the horse is bowing to me. Then the front of the horse's chest opened, and he used his mouth and head to flick the spirits at me. But Irene, you should see the Pegasus, they are so beautiful, you know me, I love horses.*

Helena told me later, *"I was on my way back from the supermarket, and the giant maidens were emptying their dresses of spirits everywhere. Then, when I came home and looked up, I saw ordinary horses galloping through the clouds, which were breathtaking. There were lots of Pegasus, and their riders made them rear so that they rose on their hind legs - their bellies opened as well, and the spirits came out of them. It's the most amazing thing I have ever seen in my life. I feel completely blessed after seeing that. I have a Pegasus tattoo. (It's true; Helena has a tattoo of a Pegasus on her back.) I think they have also collected horse spirits, Irene. They are rounding up horses in circles so that they can come through me. I can see a whole display of horses kicking and jumping. On some of the horses, the men are getting off and opening a flap in the saddle, and they are letting spirits out there. I think they're also being released from their hind area,"* she laughed. *I can see them flying from a distance, some avoiding and dodging each other in the sky and flying down. They are spectacular! They are jumping and galloping through the sky. The horses have very long manes. When I die and go to heaven, I am going to be flying one of these on the weekend. I'm going to make that deal with God that when I die, I will be allowed to ride a Pegasus."*

I wondered if the Pegasus were horse angels, spirits of horses that served in wars and if the Pegasus were rounding up their own species. The Pegasus also carried human spirits.

Millions of Horses Run Free

June 27th: The flow of horse and human spirit continued to flow through her house. After three and a half hours of sleep, she woke hearing someone say, "She's awake." Helena saw people dressed in animal skins holding sticks; they looked like chiefs of some tribe. They seemed anxious, as if they were in a rush and had a deadline. At first, they did not realize she could see them, but then she stretched and waved, and they started running away. The flow of millions of horses started again and followed them. It seemed they came to see why the horses were not going through the tunnel. Helena closed her eyes and saw millions of horses run free through a vast dusty land. They seemed happy and carefree. Nothing could go through the tunnel when Helena slept.

28th, 29th, and 30th June: This massive exodus of spirits continued over the next three days. Helena worked very hard, constantly praying and looking after her house, children, and animals. She was exhausted and desperate for it to end.

Jesus & the Prophecy of His Return

Jesus

July 1st: Helena arrived in the field and instantly heard people roar, "She is here, she is here. Release me, let me go, release me, let me go." She prayed as she walked through the field and, sitting down, noticed a dark pink wildflower. The thought struck her, *"I am like that flower, here on my own, one flower surrounded by all these spirits."* She wondered, *"Will I pick it?"* She heard the voice of Saint Andrew say, *"Yes, pick it and bring it home."* Walking back to the stable, she sat on her upturned bucket to let the flow of spirits come through. Over the last two days, she had heard them shout, *"We are walking through her. We are walking through her."* Then she heard the crowd shout, *"It's a miracle. It's a miracle. Christ is coming. Christ is coming. He's walking to the miracle girl. He is walking to the miracle girl."* Then Saint Andrew said, *"Fill your heart with the love of Christ. Fill your heart with the love of Christ."* So, Helena tried to do this, and as she did, she noticed a light in front of her was *shining bright. She felt surges of energy pulse through her body and heard the crowd chant, "Christ is coming,"* this went on for about fifteen minutes. Then Saint Andrew spoke again, saying, *"Christ is here with His disciples."* The crowd shouted, *"He is here. He is in front of you. He carries His cross on his back."*

The field was filled with light beings: nuns, priests, angels, knights, and crowds of human spirits. The field was enveloped in an ocean of mist, and within the mist were the lights of the individual spirits. Their spirit lights flashed and shone through the mist like lightning in a cloudy sky or a disco light behind a smoke machine. Then, some spirit outlines became clearer in front of her. They were the outlines of the heavenly congregation: bishops, priests, etc... then someone stood in front of her wearing a tunic, and a pair of hands opened the tunic at the chest; within it was a red heart with a gold light on top and it was pulsating. The crowd roared repeatedly, *"He is showing you His heart."* Helena saw no face, just His tunic, hands, and glowing red and gold heart. Up in the sky, there was a crucifix. They kept saying, *"He is risen. He is risen."* They lifted and dropped the crucifix repeatedly. At 9:51 pm on the audio, Jesus showed Helena His heart. I heard her say this, followed by the sound of her kicking the bucket from beneath her as she knelt before Him. The rain lashed down. The crowd shouted, *"He is walking through her."* The rain drowned out any chances of hearing the faint calls of spirit. I heard her say, *"His heart is beautiful. It is really glowing. His heart is radiating. His heart is beating. He is opening His heart to me."* The light of His heart was radiating like the sun - it wasn't a physical heart, they told her; it was His heart. What she saw was a pulsating golden light. She stayed in the field and let the crowds go through.

When I listen to this audio, I hear very little other than the rain beating down, Helena kicking the bucket from beneath her, and the description of His heart. You would think there was nothing going on at all. But for her, every field around her was filled with hysterical crowds while Jesus and His disciples walked among them - Jesus, with His cross on his back.

When she closed her eyes that night, she saw Saint Andrew carrying a cross among the crowd. Back in the garden, she saw a giant light maiden. The crowds were screaming, and Helena wondered why. She witnessed the heavenly congregation walk out of the back of the maiden's dress. They held a processional crucifix in their hand. Her back opened, and inside her back was a castle. Another giant came over and closed the back of her dress. Then she walked in through a big door - which had to be enormous. The crowd calmed down when they went back in. It was like the British royal family entering onto the balcony of Buckingham Palace and then walking back inside.

Saint Andrew & The Apostles

July 2nd: Helena voice messaged, and she was in a temper. Her voice was cracking with tiredness. She had stayed up until 1:30 am praying fervently. There was chaos in her room. Spirit walked through the house all night, and Christopher woke up and climbed into bed beside her. She had a headache, and it was 6:00 am when she was poked by a man who was responsible for getting the work done. She shouted at him for not letting her sleep and threatened to sleep for the rest of the day, asking him where would they be then. He was not happy with her, and she wasn't happy with him. She went to the sitting room, closed her eyes, and watched billions of souls fly through the portal. She couldn't bear to look at them. She hoped this would be over and she could rest, but it seemed to never end. She heard the spirit workers say, "Keep moving. Keep moving." I found it painful listening to her as she was so exhausted. I felt so sorry for her and wanted to help, but couldn't. The workers kept on repeating, "Can you see him?" They wanted her to witness Saint Andrew. This seemed to be important. But she had a hard time finding him in the crowds. The night before, she was shown Saint Andrew; he had a long grey beard and was carrying a cross. When I looked up the internet later, I saw that this is how Saint Andrew is depicted. When Helena got things like that right, it amazed me.

Arriving in the field in the afternoon, the sun was beaming down - a drastic change in weather from the previous day. The people shouted, *"The apostles are coming. The apostles are coming."* Soon, she was told, *"The apostles are here. They have His crucifix. They are showing you His crucifix that He was crucified on."*

Helena: They stood the crucifix up in front of me, and then walked around, parading it to the crowd. Then, a man wearing a tunic walked up to me. He opened the strings of the tunic displaying His heart. The crowd shouted repeatedly, *'He is showing her His heart. He is showing her His heart.* Then the heart, which had a beaming light emanating from it, was taken out of His chest and passed from one to another until it came closer to me. The crowd shouted, *"They are showing her His heart. They are showing her His heart!"*

When Helena left the field, the crowd shouted, *"She is leaving. The miracle girl is leaving,"* The crowd seemed to describe everything that went on around them as if to tell others who could not see what was going on. Helena heard, *"He is coming home. The Coming of*

155

Christ is happening or will happen again." She remembered the vision of the Sacred Heart in the tunnel and believed they were preparing her for what she was witnessing. This was true to form – *the vision was an introduction.*

Later, she messaged, *"Just imagine Irene, there are giant light beings in the sky with buckets pouring out spirits; well, that is what is happening in my garden. I know it sounds ridiculous, but this is what I see. I'm here drinking a cup of tea."* She sounded so tired and sent me a selfie - she looked terrible. She had tried to sleep but was poked and pushed, so she lay there blindfolded and prayed all day.

Back in the house, she heard, *"Christ is coming to you soon. Christ is coming to you soon. You will be so powerful."* Helena didn't feel powerful; she was exhausted. Helena asked the spirits a question. One that was bothering me. As Helena said, there were millions, if not billions, of spirits; I wondered how there could be so many. I thought before that this might be a hundred-year thing. We weren't expecting the answer she received. The spirits chanted, *"Since He has been crucified. Since He has been crucified. You are moving every soul since He has been crucified. The world will know, the world will know, it's a miracle."*

Then, the light of a crucifix shone on the wall, followed by the light of twelve apostles who appeared to walk across her wall - the one in front carrying a processional crucifix. Wearing robes with ropes around their waist, they walked to her side of the bed. And one apostle lifted his processional crucifix, and the spirits said, *"They are blessing you."* Then, a light archway appeared at the foot of her bed.

The Prophecy of His Return

July 3rd: Helena came to me for a cup of tea, then left to attend to Belle. In the field, she stood for a few minutes with her eyes closed, praying and releasing spirits. Then, a group of light beings walked toward her, and once again, the tunic opened in front of her, emanating its glowing light. This time, the light was red. It was taken out of the chest so Helena could have a closer look, and then it was put back in, followed by the closing of the tunic. The figure of the tunic-wearing man came slightly more into focus, and he wore a crown, but not a big crown like a king would wear, but a small crown. He walked away, entering a door of light. She presumed it was Jesus but couldn't make out his face. She tried to describe what happened next. He walked into the door of a castle; the castle was within a light giant, and then the giant went into a bigger castle - within, within, and within. Then, on her left side was a light church, and nuns went through the door of this church. She heard them tell her she was "*An angel of the Lord.*" Arriving home, she heard a relentless chant:

Spirit: *He is coming, He is coming.*

Jesus is coming; Jesus is coming.

He is coming to your house. Jesus is coming to your house.

Helena*: Is Jesus coming to my house? When?*

Saint Andrew: *In the next few days.*

Helena: *Who am I talking to?*

Saint Andrew: *Saint Andrew.*

Then, to her left, the arches of a church appeared, and Saint Andrew had already turned and was walking through a door of this church. She was happy and excited. She wondered why it was her that was chosen and heard a spirit say, "*She thinks she is a nobody. She doesn't know she is special. You are angels; you were chosen. He loves you.*" She questioned whether it was Jesus in the field because light beings are very faint, and it was hard to make out their features. She was sure he had a small beard like a goatee and wore a small crown. I asked her if it was a crown of thorns. But Saint Andrew answered her, "*He wasn't wearing His thorns. He wasn't wearing*

His thorns. It was a crown of gold. He was wearing a crown of gold."

They told her He was with Samuel and Bartholomew. They repeated Samuel and Bartholomew. Helena had problems pronouncing Bartholomew.

Saint Andrew said, *"You will be an angel of God when Jesus Christ will be inside you. He will not scare you. He will bless you with love".* She once again saw the light of Saint Andrew on the wall; it seemed to be Saint Andrew who was the voice.

She messaged, *"Irene, this is unbelievable. I've just seen full-size apostles walk through a large light doorway beside me in my bedroom. Well, they look like monks with the long robes and ropes around their waist."* Then, she had a vision of the interior of a church; Helena went on to explain what was happening as it was happening. *"I'm sitting on my bed. There is a carpet laid out in front of me, and there is a long line of people walking down it. There are nuns on the left and right, and people are walking down towards me. They are putting a crucifix on the aisle, and yes, they are showing me the rising again. There is a man lying on the cross, and he is raising his head. They are rubbing their hands along the cross as they raise it. All the nuns are kissing each side of his cheek. (I'm not sure who was on the cross.)* She heard, *'You will be risen and blessed. He will raise you up, and you will be blessed.'"*

In the next voicemail, Helena was in her car on her way to feed Belle. Helena said, *"Yvonne Beauvais spoke to me in a French accent;* she said, *'It is me. It is Yvonne Beauvais.'* Then I heard a female voice singing, *'He is coming. He is coming.'"*

It took me time to figure out what was happening, so I will try to make it easier to understand. Even though Helena sat on her bed, it was as if Helena was in a church, which was filling up with people and clergy. The crucifix stood at the top of the church aisle, and everyone was rubbing it and kissing both cheeks of the man lying on it. A ceremony was about to begin, but we didn't know what was happening at that moment. (And the woman singing was like a singer that we would hire to sing at a wedding or funeral). Then, Yvonne Beauvais introduced herself to Helena for the first time in nine months. They said they were going to raise Helena up when Stephen went to work.

She believed it would happen the following day. I messaged her soon after, telling her that I was experiencing tingling all over my head. (It was common when I spoke to Helena during this time. Luther said we would work in *unity,* and I felt I was energetically connected to Helena in some way or that angels stood behind me.) During this time, I would feel a distinct tingling in my head when Helena was about to call or text me. Even when writing this book, I still feel it at times; it's as if my work is being observed and noted.

Minutes later, I received another message; she was in the field crying, *"Maybe it's because Jesus was right in front of me; that's why you're experiencing tingling now. They won't let me see His face. I didn't see His face, just His body, and heart, and He held it in His hand right in front of me - the light of His heart was red and had radiant gold around it. He was right in front of me and offered it to me. I got down on my knees and blessed myself."* Helena pointed to her heart and then to Jesus to tell Him she loved him too. They had told her before, *"He won't show his face."* She continued, *"I saw Jesus taking His heart out and holding it in His hands right in front of me. Then He opened His chest and showed me His light."* She took a deep breath to calm herself and explained again. *"First, He opened His chest and showed me the light of His heart. Then He took His heart out right in front of me and offered it to me, like someone offering a piece of bread. Then, the heart was passed down from 'being' to 'being' right up in front of my face. They wanted me to have a good look at this.'* She explained further, *"They have a bright light, a glow, and it's shining bright, the brightest thing you have ever seen in your life. It's red. It's not the shape of a heart like you would think the shape of a human heart is. It's red and has a golden glow. Just think of the sun, Irene - a golden glow all around it. It's glowing, and they are holding it in their hands. It's a glowing, pulsating, and illuminating light. The Apostles are here. Saint Andrew stood in front of me and bowed. He has grey hair and a grey beard. The apostles have come from the clouds. They are showing me crucifixes again. The people in the crowd are helpful as they are telling me where to look within the mist, lights, and arched balconies."* She heard, *"He will be here in the morning when you wake. They are blessing you. They are blessing you."*

She continued, *"A door in the sky opened, and a light shone out, then a giant light-being in the sky shook a staff of light in my direction and blessed me. It's a gold crozier with light emanating from it, and he is shaking it up and down. The apostles are also blessing me. Someone said, 'It is Andrew, Bartholomew, and Simon.' (She also heard Peter). They are the three apostles who are here. Andrew is right in front of me. Bartholomew is to the right, and Simon, I think, is to the left, and they're saying they are honoring me, and he is still shaking that crozier over me. They all have one each. Everywhere I look, someone is shaking something over me."* Helena heard a clear voice and turned to see if someone human had come along. But it was a spirit very close who said, *"Their spirits are here with you."*

She continued, *"More light beings are walking down steps - one has a processional crucifix. They are shaking it at me, too. I think all the heavens are here, all the holy people are here. It's got to do with honoring and blessing me. I feel this rising-up will be in the morning. This is my third day of seeing His heart, and there is a lot going on."*

Then, in the sky ahead and slightly above her, Saint Andrew stood at an altar upon a balcony (as if he were in a church). He drank from a chalice, and someone said, *"He is drinking for His Coming."* On another balcony to her right stood priests and nuns. A nun opened a large book and then closed it. Helena said, "I don't know what this book is, but I am trying to find out. Oh! I heard it's *The Prophecy of His Return.* I think that's what I heard." On a third balcony to the left, all the apostles sat in a row.

The significance of the religious book Helena saw in her vision, the one she thought looked like the Book of Kells, was now revealed – it was to signify *The Prophecy of His Return*. I received a voice message from Helena minutes later. "This is still going on, but I'm leaving now as it's starting to rain." Another message dinged minutes later. Helena said, "I was leaving, and I heard them say, *'They want you. They want you. They are still honoring you.'* Saint Andrew stood to leave; then I saw the apostles leaving. The nuns still had the book, and the priests beside them had processional crucifixes, and they were breaking bread, making sure everyone was getting some. It was going on in a big semicircle around me.'"

They started to leave, and then Helena was allowed to leave. Helena had been leaving a mass! At that stage, Helena didn't even know it *was* a mass! She said, "I thought it was over; that is why I was leaving. There were so many people there; I thought it was three apostles, but I didn't realize there were people on the ground as well. There was a nun and a priest standing at the side of my car. I think all this is coming to an end. Irene, they said this prophecy they were discussing was in the Bible. They told me, *'The world will know; it will honor you.'*"

When Helena arrived home, she sat in her garden and watched the mass in the sky; it hadn't ended. This time, she had a Gin and Tonic in her hand.

The Prophecy of Saint Helena

Helena is Heaven Blessed

July 4th: I woke to a voice message from Helena, "'Well, I was risen. I woke at 7:00 am, and I heard, *'Jesus is in your home. He is in your house.'*'"

Again, she was shown the interior of the church. At first, she saw the altar, and her view zoomed backward, so her perspective was further away, showing its whole interior. It was the church where the carpet had been laid previously, and it was filling up with people. Everybody she'd met over the previous nine months was there. A special ceremony or event was going to take place. Herou and Luther were in attendance, as well as Catherine the Great - always noticeable because of her large dresses. Helena asked, "Luther, is that you?" We hadn't heard from him in months. He said, "Hello, Helena." Stephen heard Helena and shouted, "Tell Luther I said hello!" The congregation continued to crowd into the church. A mass took place, and they said, *'We are honoring you. You will be Saint Helena,'* and she thought, *I know that!* And they said, *'No! You will be anointed St. Helena before you die.'* Irene, they are telling me I will die a saint basically.'"

Imagine the scene - Helena lying in bed in her tiny cottage, and surrounding her was a kind of holographic church. They said they had to wait until Stephen left for work. They told her to drink water, and she could brush her hair but not eat. Stephen ate his breakfast and left for work. Suddenly, she felt a heavy force holding her down and was locked to the bed - she couldn't move. Out of Helena's body rose a purple energy that floated and transformed into Yvonne Beauvais. Yvonne walked up the carpeted aisle of the church, and everyone applauded her. Confused, Helena messaged, "So, Irene, they raised her up and not me. I was watching that, and I thought, oh! It wasn't me." Then Saint Andrew said, *'He will raise you up.*

He will raise you up.' Then Yvonne's energy or soul came back down into my body, and I saw Jesus on the wall. His hands were outstretched, rising upward. Jesus said, *'Helena, you are beautiful.'* Saint Andrew then spoke and said, *'He rose your spirit up also.'* So, my spirit was out of my body in front of Him. I could not move.'''

Helena watched the congregation leave the church, and afterward, walked into her garden looking skyward. Curtains opened, and Saint Andrew continued flicking energy upon her with his staff. She was asked to go to her bedroom alone, and Saint Andrew would come to her soon.

The next voice message from Helena was cheerful, "I'm in my bedroom. They are here, and they are filling me up with energy. It's Andrew, Bartholomew, and Simon. They are shaking their crucifixes on me, and there is an energy coming from them. As I lie here, my third eye is glowing purple. They are filling me with loving energy. The whole bedroom is filled with a purple haze, and I have pins and needles all over my body. I feel energy all around me. I went to take a photograph and look at how the photo turned out. The energy is pouring into my nose and everywhere now. Look at the photo; it looks like there is a cross on my face."

As I looked at the selfie, I saw diagonal rays of purple light shine across the top of the photo. The picture of Helena lying in bed was clouded in a haze as if someone had shaken the phone while taking the photo. I even think I see a light cross on her face. The horizontal bar goes across her eyebrow while the vertical bar goes up her nose and forehead. Is the evidence of everything Helena experienced right in front of both our faces? I showed it to two of my daughters, asking if they saw anything unusual in the photograph. But they said they didn't.

Later, angels with flowers in their hair rolled up the carpet in the church. Helena asked, "What's happening?" Saint Andrew answered. *"They are cleaning up the church. It's your church. You are an angel of God, and you will always be in a church. The church will house your spiritual energies; you will be in one for the rest of your life.*'" Later, she went to the field, and Saint Andrew was once again in the sky, flicking energy at her. Helena was feeling great; she was literally filled with energy that she felt in waves flowing through her. She took another photo in the kitchen and looked lovely, healthy, and radiant - an extreme contrast to the selfie she'd taken outside a couple of days before.

The Ending

Heaven to Hell

July 5th: Helena was delighted it was over, and she closed her eyes and saw the portal closing. She was very excited about what was to come, and so was I. I was glad this part was ending, as Helena was exhausted and had hardly slept in weeks. As the day wore on, spirits continued to speak, relaying positive messages about her future. Then, the positivity faded quickly, and the tone and content changed dramatically. Helena continued to ask questions, and the spirits continued to answer. But the voices that spoke to her did not name themselves, and there were no images or visions where she could see the person. There were no angels, heavenly beings, or realms that she could see or travel to.   But the more questions she asked, the more confused she became as the responses became unclear, erratic, and made very little sense – as if designed to confuse.

As the days went by, there were no visions, only voices that changed and became threatening and sinister. They concocted stories about her family members as if trying to turn her against them. They threatened her family in numerous ways, and she vowed to them that they would not harm her sister or any members of her family. Helena became anxious and paranoid; sleep eluded her, and she was terrified and frantic as the unidentified voices were relentless; fear consumed her, and there seemed to be no way out for her. Her behavior changed, and nothing she said made sense. She was tormented. She listened to them for twenty-four hours a day and mentally and bravely fought them.

By mid-July, Helena's husband Stephen and I admitted Helena to the Ashlin Centre at Beaumont Hospital, which provides acute care and treatment for people with mental health issues in North Dublin. She received a diagnosis of schizophrenia. To get her help, I had to tell the Doctor in the emergency room that Helena was seeing things that weren't real. I felt like Judas. I had betrayed my sister. I was crushed. What had once been heavenly had turned into hell.

July 19th: Helena voice messaged from the Ashlin Centre, "Thanks, Irene, for minding my children and taking care of everything," She sounded more like herself and wanted to come home. There was nothing to do there during the Corona pandemic, as all activities within the centre were cancelled. I encouraged her to rest, assuring her that everything was taken care of. When Helena was admitted, my husband gave me, *'The look,'* the one that said, *Really Irene? Do you see what you have done? You helped put your sister into a mental health facility. You encouraged her delusion.* I felt deeply ashamed of myself. I nodded to him without saying a word. How did I not see this? How could I let this happen to my sister? What kind of a fool was I for believing what happened was true? I was sick to my stomach. I could barely speak to Helena over the phone. I could not deal with her at all. I just wanted to be alone and wanted her to get better. I was completely confused, and my anxiety skyrocketed. I found myself constantly gripping my stomach. I was in a daze most of the time, in shock as I tried to absorb the unexpected and devastating turn of events. To whom could I turn to talk about it? The answer was as usual - no one. I went to my doctor for anxiety pills. One wasn't enough to dull the anxiety in my gut; two helped a bit.

Nine months of wonder and excitement and it had all been a dream - an illusion. Helena and I were devastated. Helena even more so as she questioned her mental health. I went to an energy healer who happened to be a counsellor and believed in the spiritual. I told him what happened - I felt I would explode if I didn't. He was probably the only person in the world who would listen to me and said he believed it was all true. Whether he was honest with me or not wasn't important; I got it off my chest.

When Helena came home two weeks later, she was still recovering from the fear of the voices - all she wanted to do was stay with her husband and sons. I was happy for her to do that, as I still wasn't in a place where I could revisit the past.

But in the weeks that followed, we went for slow walks where we tried to figure out what happened. We reviewed the previous months' events and reexamined everything, asking ourselves the same questions repeatedly. Was it real? Did it happen? If the voices at the end terrified her and she really believed they were real, then wasn't it possible that the rest wasn't real either? Our minds were filled with doubt. If I continued to doubt her, that meant Helena would have no one to believe in her, and she would have to accept that she had mental health issues. I felt so sorry for her.

On August 27th, Helena received a channel from a woman who said her name was Gertrude. Gertrude informed Helena that she was her new guide. "How come I can't see you?" Asked Helena. Gertrude answered *You have elevated past the point where you were before; I'm right outside your door. Plans for you in time, you will see, my dear, when everything becomes clear. Books and books and books, my dear. You will be an expert in your field. Wait, and you will see, we will not reveal this to ye. Something in you has to wither and die.'''*

When Helena became ill so suddenly, it was like a bomb had gone off, and we were shell-shocked and stunned. But as the months passed and the smoke began to clear, there were aspects of her experiences that we couldn't reconcile. For example, when I asked Luther a question, he answered. Yvonne Beauvais was a real person! I also found a web page stating Yvonne wanted to save souls. Helena spoke about characteristics of the Hierarchy *before* they told her their identity; for example, with Henry V, she said, "This man has a fiery spirit; you should feel the power of him!" (Henry V was known and celebrated as one of the greatest warrior kings of medieval England.) His wife introduced herself as Catherine (which I found out later was Catherine of Valois). Describing Henry VIII, Helena said, "There is a big burly man on a throne in armor; he is a big, big guy!" (Henry VIII was huge!) When Helena pronounced Catherine of Aragón's name, she pronounced it the Spanish way, sounding like Catalin. And then there was King Solomon, whom Helena had never heard of either, and Catherine the Great in her big dresses!

167

Most importantly, the bit that I could not deny was when I felt the angel's energy while Michelle simultaneously sent me a text with a message from an angel. But if all this really happened, why did the celestials abandon us? Why would they let Helena go through the hell that she went through? These questions tied us up in knots. I decided to review the WhatsApp audios and texts and realized there was so much more, like the channels in rhyme and their messages about global warming. The people were all introduced to Helena: Luther, Herou, The Hierarchy, and the knights & maidens in order of how they appeared. Everything was in order from beginning to end, culminating with a mass and honors. Helena hadn't understood half of what she was seeing - she spoke out of her mouth everything she saw as she saw it. She was also coherent and went about her daily life normally for nine months. Then, when the portal closed and they disconnected, there was instant confusion and disorder.

Conclusion

The events Helena experienced were astonishing from beginning to end, but the experiences in the final days transcended them all. They concluded with a mass, where Saint Andrew drank for *'His Coming,'* and a nun announced *The Prophecy of His Return.* They also said the prophecy was in the Bible. I have checked the internet for information on Bible prophecies, wondering if any of them resonated with Helena's experiences. The nearest thing that correlates to it that I can see is the prophecy of the *Second Coming of Jesus.* Words like 'Rapture,' Tribulation,' and 'End Times' flash across my screen, and I'm reminded of the celestial messages about the End of the World. The Russian invasion of Ukraine, Israel declaring war, and the seemingly unending natural disasters provide a convincing backdrop to their message.

Helena and I are neither eschatologists nor psychiatrists; we're housewives trying to make sense of this. Did Helena witness something biblical? Or was it some sort of psychosis? Having heard nothing from the spirit world since August 2020, Helena and I walk around like the deceased she released as if *we're* in some 'unseen dimension' wondering what happened? What to do next? Or if we should *do* anything. What we are left with are the audios chronicling these events, which I was asked to document. In the absence of further instruction from spirit, I have chosen to write this book, hoping I'm making the right decision. What will come of this? I don't know, and I am scared to tell you the truth. God said we signed a contract that we are not to forget! I don't remember signing anything, but I'm not taking any chances.

I asked Helena for any thoughts or words she would like to add to the conclusion of this book. Through her tears, she told me that she grieves daily. She feels loss and sadness at losing the ability to see the unseen: palaces, heavenly gardens, beautiful worlds, the colours of God's heart, and the dazzling beauty of heavenly beings. To have been able to talk to our deceased mother and old friends who died young and to have laughed with them once more, all with such incredible ease that she didn't then appreciate. She mourns the fact that she may never see them again until God calls her home. She meditates daily and still sees the colours, but for the first time since she was a teenager, she does not experience *any* type of spiritual presence or activity around her - only silence and peace. Ironically, Helena now wishes they were back.

After her time in the Ashlin centre, Helena hadn't the same enthusiasm for life as she had before and decided to rid her life of excess stress; this meant first letting go of her beloved Belle. It was a hard decision, and she was heartbroken. Unfortunately, on New Year's Eve 2020, while walking her dog Hank (whose soothing snoring is heard in many of the audios), he ran too far ahead on one of Ireland's frostiest days, disappearing only to be found dead on a beach miles away. She had lost her little 'earth angel.' If that wasn't enough, her marriage recently dissolved. Helena now seems to be a different person, and instead of working constantly, she rests and has become quieter and a little subdued. She has left her cottage and is living quietly in the country. I wondered about Gertrude's final message, "Something in you has to wither and die." Is it the withering away of the old Helena? As regards Helena's physical health, she's had no severe pain since her manipulation and doesn't cry while turning or moving; she still has muscle stiffness but has been able to come off a very potent painkiller.

With COVID lockdowns and the anticlimax of our experiences, I, too, feel changed. An impatient, creative person who like a child, gets distracted easily, I find playing back audios, documenting, and editing the material laborious work. It takes great persistence and perseverance - traits that are not in my nature but ones I find I am cultivating. I go through a rollercoaster of emotions when I read the material: in awe one moment, then despair seconds later. It would help if I could discuss the content objectively with someone. My husband, although a man of faith, had a hard time believing what I was trying to tell him, so I gave up. I can't blame him; I hardly believe it myself, but I'm compelled to write the book, and as always, he supports me. So, like Helena, I am forced to be patient and wait, wondering what, if anything, will unfold.

Helena and I talk regularly, and I try to keep her spirits up by telling her the book is coming along and that I believe all she experienced was true. Some days, I'm filled with doubt because it is so unbelievable – even to us, but I listen to the audios and read what I've documented, and it reminds me that these nine months of experiences really happened. If we didn't have the audios, we could easily believe it was all a dream. Either way, it is one amazing story.

One Final Note

In the final days of Helena's experiences, she witnessed nuns passing a St. Brigid's cross to one another. This cross is very distinctive, especially to Irish Catholics, as there wasn't a child in primary school in Ireland who didn't make one on St. Brigid's day – February 1st. St. Brigid's cross is typically made of rushes or straw. It has four arms that are linked at the ends and have a woven square in the centre. To Christians, it symbolises the saving grace of God through Jesus Christ. It is said that Brigid made it and gave it to a chieftain on his deathbed, and in explaining its meaning, it calmed his soul and he asked to be baptised before he died. St. Brigid then became Ireland's female patron saint. I have wondered why Helena was shown this cross; its characteristics set it apart from any other crosses or crucifixes she had seen. Could it be something to do with baptism? Or that all this happened in Ireland? Or could this have been a symbolic prediction? Because on February 7th, 2022, the Irish government signed into law a new public holiday - St. Brigid's Day! No one knew this was coming. Was this just a coincidence? Or were the celestials telling us two years before that St. Brigid would have her day.

Helena's Releasing Prayer

Go, dear ones; you are loved, blessed, healed, blessed, healed and forgiven. You are one with your own higher selves. You are filled and surrounded by the cosmic Christ's love. I call upon Jesus to take you to your own special place. A place of healing, love, joy, abundance, hope, charity, and forgiveness. Go with Jesus. Go now, and so it is, three multiplexes by an infinite number of times, by an infinite number of times, to beyond the beyond.

About the Author

Irene Lawlor lives in Dublin, Ireland with her husband, daughters, and dog Ginger. An active mother, secretary, and amateur actor, she was dramatically catapulted into a more subdued lifestyle in 2006, when she suffered a cardiac arrest while pregnant and was resuscitated. Three months later it happened again - miraculously, she and her baby survived; someone watched over them. The fatigue that comes with heart failure, endless tachycardias and severe shocks from her implantable defibrillator forced her to find a different outlet for her creativity. Someone suggested writing and in 2013 she self-published her debut novel *Discovering Ireland*, a romantic comedy set in... you guessed, Ireland! Like most people after receiving a life-changing diagnosis, she asked "Why me?" She now believes that it was part of a pre-birth plan to deconstruct her life, so she'd learn to write - *Discovering Ireland* was the practice run, *The Girl the God Fell To* was the goal. Now in advanced heart failure Irene is waiting for another miracle – a new heart.

Glossary

Angel: A supernatural being often depicted as a benevolent celestial intermediary between God and humanity in various religions. A messenger from God.

Archangel: An angel of high rank. Referenced in this book are Raphael, Gabriel, Uriel, and Michael.

Astral body: A subtle body vibrating at a higher frequency than the physical body, posited by many to be an intermediate between the intelligent soul and the mental body. It is believed that a living being has an astral body as well as a physical one.

Astral plane or world: Another dimension that exists above the physical plane or world. It has different levels, from high to low. It's believed to be populated by spirits and is a replica of the physical world.

Astral projection: (or astral travel) is a term used in esotericism to describe an intentional out-of-body experience (OBE) that assumes the existence of a soul called an " astral body " that is separate from the physical body and capable of travelling outside it throughout the universe.

Aura: An invisible electromagnetic force field that emanates from people, plants, and animals. According to spiritual beliefs, an aura or human energy field is a coloured emanation. It reflects health, thoughts, emotions, and other information while protecting the individual from outside negative influences, including discarnate spirits.

*Book of Kells: An illuminated manuscript and Celtic Gospel book in Latin containing the four Gospels of the New Testament.

Channelling: Allowing a spirit from the higher planes to manifest through a medium's physical body, most commonly by speaking or writing. Normally conveying messages of love and wisdom.

Clairaudience: The ability to psychically hear what lies beyond physical sound.

Clairsentience: The ability of a person to acquire psychic knowledge by means of feeling.

Clairvoyance: The ability to psychically see what lies beyond normal sight.

Consciousness: The state of being awake and aware of one's surroundings.

Discarnate: A spirit who is trapped in the physical world, i.e., not the higher planes, without his or her physical body.

Earthbound: A condition of remaining in the physical world as a spirit after the death of the body because of not having made a successful transition into the higher realms. According to esoteric theory, and earthbound spirit is actually trapped in the lower astral plane.

Knight: A person granted an honorary title of knighthood by a head of state or representative for service to the monarch, the church, or the country, especially in a military capacity, as a mounted soldier in Armor.

Knight of the Light: The spirit of a knight who is honoured by God to fight for HIM and protect the light of spiritual beings and heavenly places from the darkness. My definition.

Medium: A person who is sensitive psychically and able to communicate with spirits and produce manifestations.

Near Death Experience: An unusual experience taking place on the brink of death and recounted by a person on recovery, typically an out-of-body experience or a vision of a tunnel of light.

Out-of-Body-Experience OBE: The spirit travels while still connected to the physical body by the "silver cord," sometimes referred to as astral projection or soul travel.

Parallel Universe: (In quantum mechanics) a universe theorized as existing alongside our own, although undetectable. The concept of parallel universes is not widely accepted in physics but is gaining ground.

Reincarnation: The return to physical existence by the soul in repeated existences.

*Remote Viewing: The ability to acquire accurate information about a distant or non-local place, person, or event without using your physical senses or any other obvious means. It's sometimes called "second sight" and is a trained skill that the average person can learn to do.

Soul: The spiritual or immaterial part of a human being or animal, regarded as immortal.

Spirit: The immaterial intelligent or sentient part of a person. The vital essence is animating the body or mediating between body and soul.

Spirit Guides: Highly evolved souls from the spirit world who offer help to living people. They can give them guidance and aid.

Spirit World: The realm of life which is populated by spirits who have gone into the Light and made a successful transition from the physical world. It is a place of existence generally regarded as vibrating at a higher frequency than the physical world.

Spirit Realm: A junction where the physical domain of the universe and the spirit world interact together.

Telepathy: The psychic transmission and reception of thoughts.

Third Eye: The third eye is a mystical and esoteric concept of a speculative invisible eye, which provides perception beyond ordinary sight. In certain spiritual traditions, the third eye is the gate that leads the followers within to inner realms and spaces of higher consciousness.

Trance: A sleep-like state in which there is a lessening of consciousness. It can vary from slight to extremely deep. It can be hypnotic or nonhypnotic.

Tunnel of light: An illuminated, energetic tunnel-like passageway or 'spiritual highway' that allows the human spirit or astral body to transition from the physical world to the spiritual world. It is commonly reported by people who have had Near Death Experiences. It's also said to allow the spirit access to other dimensions.

www.ingramcontent.com/pod-product-compliance
Lightning Source LLC
Chambersburg PA
CBHW071854020426
42331CB00010B/2517

* 9 7 8 0 9 5 7 4 1 4 3 6 5 *